Do Not Lose Heart

Resources by Dave Dravecky

Dave Dravecky (Today's Heroes) (with Tim Stafford)

Resources by Jan Dravecky

A Joy I'd Never Known (with Connie Neal)

Resources by Dave and Jan Dravecky

Do Not Lose Heart (with Steve Halliday)
Glimpses of Heaven (with Amanda Sorenson)

Dave and Jan Dravecky

with Steve Halliday

Cover Illustration by Thomas Kinkade

Do Not Lose Heart

Meditations of Encouragement and Comfort

ZONDERVAN™

GRAND RAPIDS, MICHIGAN 49530

ZONDERVAN™

Do Not Lose Heart
Text copyright © 1998 by David and Janice Dravecky
Cover Illustration copyright © 1998 Thomas Kinkade, Media Arts Group, Inc.

Requests for information should be addressed to:

Zondervan, *Grand Rapids, Michigan 49530*

Library of Congress Cataloging-in-Publication Data

Dravecky, Dave.
    Do not lose heart : devotions of encouragement and comfort / Dave and
Jan Dravecky.
        p.   cm.
    Includes bibliographical references.
    ISBN: 0-310-24043-3 (softcover)
    1. Consolation.   2. Encouragement—Religious aspects—Christianity—
Meditations. 3. Hope—Religious aspects—Christianity—Meditations. 4.
Suffering—Religious aspects—Christianity—Meditations. I. Dravecky, Jan.
II. Title.
BV4905.2.D73   1998
242'.4—dc21   97-34171

Published in association with the literary agency of Alive Communications, Inc., 7680 Goddard Street, Suite 200, Colorado Springs, CO 80920.

Interior design by Sherri L. Hoffman

Printed in the United States of America

02 03 04 05 06 /❖ DC/ 10 9 8 7 6 5 4 3

Contents

From the Authors and the Artist

We are very pleased and thankful to Thomas Kinkade, the Painter of Light, for his participation in this project and for graciously allowing us the use of his inspiring work on the cover. Our prayer is that its beauty, serenity, and simplicity permeate your soul with the peace of God's love.

—Dave and Jan Dravecky

It is a pleasure to partner with Dave and Jan on this book, as they bring encouragement and comfort into the lives of those who hurt. I believe God has called me to share his peace, joy, and hope through my paintings. May you be drawn into the comforting light of our heavenly Father as you read through these pages.

—Thomas Kinkade

Acknowledgments

From the very beginning this book has been a labor of love for my wife, Jan. I have contributed, but, in reality, she deserves all the credit for the final product. Of course, she had lots of help.

We wouldn't have been able to do this project had it not been for the hard work of our literary agent, Rick Christian, and his staff at Alive Communications. Rick once again paired us up with Zondervan, our longtime publisher. Rick, we are indebted to you for your hard work—but most of all, we are grateful for your friendship.

In Zondervan we feel we have one of the best publishers around. The professionals there have become more than just business partners; they have become our friends. To Bruce Ryskamp, Scott Bolinder, John Sloan, and the entire company: Thank you for believing in us and helping us to fulfill what God has been doing through this incredible story he has entrusted to us.

Steve Halliday has worked with us on the writing of this book and we thank God for allowing this man to cross our path. Steve, your gifts and talents, as well as your understanding of suffering, have allowed this book to be all Jan and I hoped it could be (and more). Not only do we appreciate working with you, but we also are grateful for the new friendship that has begun.

So many others have contributed their stories, their prayers, their wisdom, and their insight to this project. For fear of forgetting someone, I won't mention all your names—but Jan and I thank you all from the bottom of our hearts.

Last, but not least, to the entire staff at Outreach of Hope: We thank you for giving us the freedom to devote the time necessary to bring this project to completion. We love you all very much and can't tell you enough how grateful we are that God has allowed each of you to come alongside Jan and me in providing hope and encouragement to those suffering with cancer and amputation.

This project was born out of a realization that people who suffer physically, including those with cancer, need written resources to help them cope with their circumstances. This is the first of four projects we are working on to help meet this need; so once again, to all those who continue to walk with us on the journey of suffering, we hope you will be encouraged. And if you happen to be thinking of us, please pray that God will continue to guide and direct everyone involved with this work.

In his precious love,
Dave Dravecky

Introduction

Gaining an Eternal Perspective

This may be one of the more unusual devotionals you'll ever read. Most of those we've enjoyed are intended to give an uplifting thought for the day or provide a brief, inspiring story suitable to start the morning. We're grateful for such books and we have benefited from many of them.

But what do you read when things aren't going so well in your life and you don't want to hear yet another happily-ever-after ending? What do you pick up when you need to hear the truth about life in a fallen world and about how to get through it intact? Where do you turn when you need a rock-solid word from God about dealing with the disappointments and adversities of life?

Jan and I first started asking those questions about a decade ago when I was a pitcher for the San Francisco Giants. In 1988 I was at the height of my professional baseball career when a tumor was discovered in my left arm (my pitching arm). The tumor and half of my deltoid muscle were removed quickly and doctors told me that, barring a miracle, I would never pitch again. But on August 10, 1989, that "miracle" occurred and I pitched in a 4–3 win against the Cincinnati Reds. Just five days later, however, while pitching to Tim Raines of the Montreal Expos, my arm snapped in mid-pitch and we discovered that the cancer had returned. I never pitched again. Two major surgeries and a battery of radiation treatments later, doctors amputated my left arm and left shoulder. It was June 18, 1991.

The loss of my baseball career and left arm was bad enough, but neither Jan nor I was prepared for the fear, doubt, anger, confusion, and deep anxiety that both accompanied and followed my medical battle. Jan descended into a dark depression that almost consumed her. I was not much better off. And yet both of us were Christians. How could this be happening to us? What had we done to deserve this? Where was God in all of our trials?

Eventually, with the help of family, friends, health professionals, and spiritual counselors, we began to emerge from the darkness and sought ways to help others who found themselves walking through the lonely valley we had just traveled. In August 1991 we founded Dave Dravecky's Outreach of Hope, an organization devoted to providing hope and encouragement through the gospel of Jesus Christ to those suffering from cancer and amputation. These days we send out hundreds of care packages and make thousands of phone calls each month to people in pain. We are always on the lookout for helpful materials to send to these dear friends, but we were never able to find a book that would offer bite-sized nuggets from God's Word designed to help readers cope with their suffering by focusing their attention on the eternal hope of the gospel.

This book is our humble attempt to help meet that need. Our aim is to point readers to an eternal perspective rooted in God's faithfulness as proclaimed in his Word. We want to help others discover, as we did, that our Father is not only a God of the mountaintop but also Lord of the valley (see 1 Kings 20:26–30). To be honest, we are tired of taking calls from people devastated by "friends" who have told them they are suffering or loved ones have died because they lack faith or because they (or even an ancestor!)

have grievously sinned. Should the message of the gospel cause someone in pain to feel worse? We categorically reject that notion. This book is our effort to say that while suffering and pain are a real and ongoing part of life in this fallen world, they will not have the final word. God has not promised to exempt believers from hardship and affliction, but he has pledged to redeem all of their pain and suffering and to reward their faithful endurance with pleasures at his right hand forevermore.

A passage that has loomed large in our understanding of this truth is 2 Cor. 4:16–18, which declares:

> Therefore we do not lose heart. Though outwardly we are wasting away, yet inwardly we are being renewed day by day. For our light and momentary troubles are achieving for us an eternal glory that far outweighs them all. So we fix our eyes not on what is seen, but on what is unseen. For what is seen is temporary, but what is unseen is eternal.

I quoted this passage at the conclusion of my previous two books, *When You Can't Come Back* and *The Worth of a Man*. This encouraging text tells me that although I should expect to suffer in this world, I don't have to lose heart. It insists that if I will only focus on the promised glories to come, I can not only endure my present pain but, day by day, I can be renewed within.

These words of the apostle Paul have been so crucial for Jan and me that we decided to use them as the framework for the book you hold in your hands. Each of the seven sections in this devotional are focused on one part of this text, on one component of its encouraging message. As you walk through the following pages with us, you will see that its landscape changes from rolling hills to deep valleys to soaring mountaintops. As we said, our God is a God of the valleys as well as the mountains; that truth is reflected in the readings to come. We have tried hard to speak the truth without flinching, yet always to fix our eyes and our hopes on the never-changing goodness and faithfulness of almighty God.

We suggest that you chew on each reading before moving on to the next. Don't try to read everything at once; pause regularly to allow the truths of God's Word to penetrate your soul and invigorate your spirit.

Our message throughout is the same: Do not lose heart! If we can help at least one struggling child of God to find hope and encouragement in the midst of difficult circumstances, we will have considered our labors well spent.

Now to him who is able to do immeasurably more than all we ask or imagine, according to his power that is at work within us, to him be glory in the church and in Christ Jesus throughout all generations, for ever and ever! Amen.

Do Not Lose Heart

One
Encouragement

"Therefore we do not lose heart"

God doesn't command us to stay encouraged without giving us a reason to do so. He knows there is plenty in life to cause even the stoutest soul to lose heart. Calamities and mishaps and disease and accidents and foul play and a thousand other devastations can pulverize our lives at any moment. Life in this fallen world has countless nasty ways of causing us to lose heart.

But God is greater than any calamity, mightier than any disaster. When Paul says, "*Therefore* we do not lose heart," he is thinking back in verse 14 to an irresistible reason for staying encouraged: "We know that the one who raised the Lord Jesus from the dead will also raise us with Jesus and present us with you in his presence."

Death does not have the final say—Jesus does! And so long as we are connected to Jesus by faith, death has no more say over us than it did over him. Truly, this is the most powerful reason in the universe for taking heart, no matter what happens. God wins! And we win with him.

The Key to Conquering Fear

I sought the LORD, and he answered me;
he delivered me from all my fears.

—Psalm 34:4

———

Nothing can cause us to lose heart more quickly than fear. And nothing strikes fear into our hearts more than death.

"When I began radiation treatment for my cancer," wrote one man, "I discovered what it was like to walk through the valley of the shadow of death. As I spent weeks without eating solid food, I began to realize that the physical and emotional trauma coming my way could only be met by taking the hand of the Lord and walking with him. Even so, being led through the valley of the shadow is frightening. Its uncertainties keep you alert to every changing scenario. I began to cling to every nuance of the doctors' words, shrugs, and grimaces; I experienced the full range of emotions that go with a life-threatening illness. I wept as I saw my utter need to depend on God. The fear of the unknown often gripped me."[1]

That's what the fear of death can do to us. Its icy fingers touch us all, old or young, rich or poor, black or white, clergy or layperson. The man quoted above, in fact, pastors a large, influential church. And yet he was afraid. Fear is a universal human response to death.

I battled the same fear when I was diagnosed with cancer. I couldn't bear the thought of having to leave behind my kids, my wife, my life. Something deep within me told me that death is not natural. I fought against it as if it were a foreign enemy and, in a sense, it is. Ecclesiastes 3:11 tells us that God has placed eternity into the heart of every person. We so long for life on earth to go on that we resist heaven, the true home Jesus has prepared for us. So we struggle. On one hand we are scared, on the other hand there is heaven. We wrestle back and forth between the two.

It is certain that fear will stalk every human heart. So when we feel its clammy grip, what can we do? How can we prevent it from causing us to lose heart?

The first thing we must do is to face our fears, whatever they might be. A small example from my early baseball career illustrates what I mean.

When I was first called up to the big leagues, my first eight to ten days as a San Diego Padre were a nightmare. I struggled so badly that management was toying with sending me back to Triple-A ball. We were in Los Angeles preparing to play the Dodgers, and Jan came up with our daughter, Tiffany, to stay with me at the hotel. After the first game of that series I returned to our room, obviously upset. But when Jan asked me what was wrong, I replied, "Nothing. I'm fine." Of course, deep down inside I was scared to death. Finally I blurted out, "Jan, I'm scared. I'm afraid. Everyone who comes to the plate is like Babe Ruth. I don't know whether I can pitch at this level."

With that, the dam was broken. By facing my fears and openly admitting them, I was freed to move forward as a baseball player to go out and pitch to the best of my ability. And the worst that could happen? We'd return to Triple-A ball in Hawaii, where all our friends were. Strengthened by that new outlook, I took the mound with confidence and went on to a satisfying major league career.

"But that's just baseball," you might rightly be saying. "What about the biggest fear of all—the fear of death?" I discovered the same process works there, too. I had to face my fear of dying, admit it, and go from there. And the worst that could happen? I'd take up residence in heaven, where my Savior Jesus is.

Don't get the wrong idea, however. While it was that conviction that finally won out over my fears, only after a long and intense battle did I see the truth of something C. S. Lewis wrote in *A Grief Observed*: "You never know how much you really believe anything until its truth or falsehood becomes a matter of life and death to you."[2]

The ultimate question was, did I really believe God's promises, such as the one in Hebrews 2:14–15? That text reads:

> Since the children have flesh and blood, he too shared in their humanity so that by his death he might destroy him who holds the power of death—that is, the devil—and free those who all their lives were held in slavery by their fear of death.

Did I really believe God when he said:

> Fear not, for I have redeemed you; I have summoned you by name; you are mine. When you pass through the waters, I will be with you; and when you pass through the rivers, they will not sweep over you. When you walk through the fire, you will not be burned; the flames will not set you ablaze. For I am the LORD, your God, the Holy One of Israel, your Savior. (Isa. 43:1–3)

Only after a prolonged and grueling struggle did I at last realize that I really did believe those things. No matter how things turned out, I had the assurance of going to heaven. In that way, my fear of death actually led me into a deeper place with God and I felt his embrace as never before.

I am not the only one to make this discovery. A woman named Margie Norton made the same journey I did, except that her trip took her further than mine has. Today Margie has firsthand knowledge of heaven. Just before she died of brain cancer, she sensed the Lord was about to call her home.

When it was time, she told her husband that she needed to go to the hospital. When she was in the hospital, her children and husband gathered around the bed and prayed for her. As they left her, they said, "Well, we'll see you tomorrow, Mom." She responded by saying, "You won't find much."

As soon as they left, she took a shower and put on her brand-new nightgown. The nurse happened to come in just as she was getting back in bed, and said, "My, how pretty you look! You're all dressed up to go someplace. Where are you going?"

"I'm going to meet my King," Margie replied.

Then she died and did meet her King. That's victory! That's death that has no sting![3]

Did Margie fear death? I'm sure she did, to a point. But when you know you're going to see Jesus, not even death has the final word. As Amado Nervo has written, "If you love God, you will fear nothing and no one because you can lose nothing, and all the forces of the cosmos will be impotent to take your heritage."

———

People in all ages of history have fought their fears in one way or another, but the only thing that really conquers fear is faith in the Lord: "I will trust and not be afraid" (Isa. 12:2). Only he who can say, "The Lord is my strength," can say, "Of whom shall I be afraid?"[4]

—Alexander MacLaren

Notes

1. John Wimber, "Signs, Wonders, & Cancer," *Christianity Today* 40, no. 11 (October 7, 1996): 50.

2. C. S. Lewis, *A Grief Observed* (New York: Bantam, 1976), 25.

3. Wimber, "Signs, Wonders, & Cancer," 51.

4. *Who Said It?* (Chicago: Moody Press, 1994), 196–97.

A Sight That Gives Strength

Consider him who endured such opposition from sinful
men, so that you will not grow weary and lose heart.

—Hebrews 12:3

I met Terry several years ago. She was an avid baseball fan and
especially loved the San Francisco Giants. She lived in the Bay
area and had followed my career and illness with great interest—
not only because she adored the Grand Old Game but because she
was battling a terminal case of cancer.

I got her on the phone one day to try to encourage her in the
deadly struggle she faced. We talked about our mutual interests and
the excitement of major league baseball, as well as the highs and
lows of being a Giants fan. In the middle of our conversation the
course of our discussion suddenly changed, and we began talking
about her difficult battle against cancer. I don't recall much of what
I said, but I remember vividly what she told me.

"The one thing that gets me through this as I lie here in my
hospital bed," she declared, "is knowing every morning that, if God
once more allows me to open my eyes, the first thing I'll see is a
picture of Jesus hanging on the wall at the foot of my bed. When
I see that picture of Jesus, somehow I get the strength to make it
through another day."

For someone who knows that, there's not a whole lot more that can be said. Terry discovered in her pain what all of us should remember every day of our lives: The way to get through the trials and difficulties of life is by looking to Jesus.

But why? Why should this be any help at all?

The writer of the book of Hebrews gives us the answer: "Consider him who endured such opposition from sinful men, so that you will not grow weary and lose heart," he wrote. So let's do that for a moment. Let's "consider him." What is it about Jesus that will help us to keep going and not lose heart when we face trials of whatever sort?

First, it's helpful for me to consider that he himself did not lose heart. Of what use would he be to me in my affliction if, in the midst of his own troubles, he caved? Thank God, he didn't. He wasn't dragged, kicking and screaming, to the cross. He *chose* it. "I lay down my life—only to take it up again," he said. "No one takes it from me, but I lay it down of my own accord" (John 10:17–18). He never wavered from his course, even when given the opportunity. When Peter tried to thwart his arrest in the Garden of Gethsemane, Jesus commanded him, "Put your sword away! Shall I not drink the cup the Father has given me?" (John 18:11). When the Roman governor Pilate suggested it was up to him whether Jesus lived or died, the Master replied, "You would have no power over me if it were not given to you from above" (John 19:11). Even in his last few excruciating moments on the cross, Jesus showed his unbroken spirit. He forgave those who crucified him. He welcomed a dying thief to his new home in heaven. He arranged for the care of his widowed mother. Jesus never lost heart, even as he left this world with the shout, "Father, into your hands I commit my spirit" (Luke 23:46).

Second, it encourages me to keep going in my trials when I consider how infinitely greater his sufferings were. No one ever knew suffering as Jesus knew it. His physical suffering was horrible enough—read a medical description of what happens during crucifixion sometime, if you can stand it—but many others in history have been put to death in exactly the same way. What made Jesus' death so incomparably worse than any other was that God placed on him—a man who had never known even a moment of sin's contamination—the entire vile volume of the sin of the whole world. "God made him who had no sin to be sin for us, so that in him we might become the righteousness of God," Paul wrote in 2 Corinthians 5:21. As one commentator has written:

> Christ has thus become His people's supreme inspirer of faith. When they become weary on the way, and grow faint at heart because there seems no end to the trials they have to endure, let them consider Him. He suffered uncomplainingly the hostility and malevolence of sinful men; the recipients of this epistle [Hebrews] had not been called upon to endure anything like their Master's sufferings.[1]

Martin Luther, the great Reformer, would say this even more forcefully. "Our suffering is not worthy the name of suffering," he wrote. "When I consider my crosses, tribulations, and temptations, I shame myself almost to death, thinking what are they in comparison of the sufferings of my blessed Saviour Christ Jesus."[2] And R. C. Sproul joins in the chorus when he says, "No one was ever called by God to greater suffering than that suffering to which God called His only begotten son. Our Savior was a suffering Savior. He went before us into the uncharted land of agony and death."[3]

When suffering invades their lives, many complain, "God doesn't understand!" But he does. He understands it far better than we do. Our Savior suffered vastly more than we will ever begin to grasp—and he did it for our sake.

Last, I am helped to endure my trials when I consider how Jesus endured his own: ". . . who for the joy set before him endured the cross" (Heb. 12:2). Jesus looked ahead to what his sufferings would accomplish, and great joy gripped his soul. He endured for the joy of completing the Father's will for him. He endured for the joy he would feel at his resurrection and exaltation. And he endured for the joy of soon being able to present cleansed believers to the Father in glory. Jesus did not "enjoy" the cross, but he was able to endure it for the joy set before him.

I'm not sure how much of all this Terry understood as she gazed morning after morning at a picture of Jesus hanging on the wall at the foot of her bed, but she obviously understood enough. When she considered Jesus, she took heart and was able to endure. And so can we.

Notes

1. F. F. Bruce, *The New International Commentary on the New Testament: Hebrews* (Grand Rapids: Eerdmans, 1964), 355.

2. Frank Mead, *12,000 Religious Quotations* (Grand Rapids: Baker, 1994), 361.

3. R. C. Sproul, *Surprised by Suffering* (Orlando: Ligonier Ministries).

Praying to the God Who Hears

You hear, O LORD, the desire of the afflicted;

you encourage them, and you listen to their cry.

—Psalm 10:17

One of the most difficult activities for suffering men and women to engage in is prayer. When you are in pain, it often seems that all your prayers just bounce off the ceiling. You cry out, but there seems to be no answer. And after you have lived with the silence for a while, your own voice often grows quiet.

Dave and I both struggled with this during our hard times. Being the analytical person that I am, I found it difficult to pray when I understood that God knew everything already. What could I tell him that he didn't already know? And besides, when I did pray, I could seldom detect an answer or even sense that God was listening.

In our work at the Outreach of Hope, we deal with a lot of hurting people who feel the same way. Why pray when God doesn't answer? Why pray when, apparently, he doesn't hear? Why pray when our prayers seem to rise no higher than a couple of feet above our heads?

The answer Dave and I now give can be boiled down to one thing: We pray because God tells us to pray and he promises that he both hears and answers our prayers.

It comes down to choosing to believe what God tells us in his Word. And he tells us a lot about praying! He says things like, "O people of Zion, who live in Jerusalem, you will weep no more. How gracious he will be when you cry for help! As soon as he hears, he will answer you" (Isa. 30:19). He tells us, "Do not be anxious about anything, but in everything, by prayer and petition, with thanksgiving, present your requests to God. And the peace of God, which transcends all understanding, will guard your hearts and your minds in Christ Jesus" (Phil. 4:6–7). And he takes special delight to assure us, "We do not have a high priest who is unable to sympathize with our weaknesses, but we have one [Jesus] who has been tempted in every way, just as we are—yet was without sin. Let us then approach the throne of grace with confidence, so that we may receive mercy and find grace to help us in our time of need" (Heb. 4:15–16).

All of these passages, and hundreds more like them, encourage and urge and command us to take our deepest concerns to God, who promises to hear our prayers and come to our aid. God knows that when we are in greatest distress we are in greatest danger of doubting his goodness. Jesus understood this completely. You can almost hear the pleading tone of his voice when he asked, "Which of you, if his son asks for bread, will give him a stone? Or if he asks for a fish, will give him a snake? If you, then, though you are evil, know how to give good gifts to your children, how much more will your Father in heaven give good gifts to those who ask him!" (Mat. 7:9–11).

A great preacher from a bygone era once asked his audience, "Did any of you parents ever hear your child wake from sleep with some panic-fear and shriek the mother's name through the darkness? Was not that a more powerful appeal than all words? And, depend upon it, that the soul which cries aloud on God, 'The God and Father of our Lord Jesus Christ,' though it have 'no language but a cry,' will never call in vain."[1]

When his children pray to him, God does hear and he does answer. Simply because God does not answer all of our prayers in the way we would like them to be answered does not mean that there has been no answer. We must remember that, just as a parent must sometimes say "no" to a child, so must God sometimes say "no" to us. While this may cause us grief (as our own "no" does to our children), yet this negative answer is for our good, whether we understand it or not. As C. S. Lewis has said, "I must often be glad that certain past prayers of my own were not granted."[2] Who, if they are honest, cannot say "Amen" to that? I recall how Ruth Bell Graham, the wife of world-famous evangelist Billy Graham, once said, "If God had answered every prayer of mine, I would have married the wrong man seven times." Author and pastor Don Baker has suggested there may be at least six reasons why our prayers seem to go unanswered:

1. We don't deserve the answer yet.
2. We need to learn something first.
3. It isn't the right time yet.
4. It's not what we really want.
5. It's not what we really need.
6. God wants to give us something better.

I have learned through my struggles that after I have brought a matter to God in prayer, I can release it and know that he is in charge of it. I do not have to worry about it anymore. Oh, I will continue to pray for that concern—Jesus also taught us that we "should always pray and not give up" (Luke 18:1)—but the answer, whatever it may be, is in his hands. I am confident that the psalmist was right when he wrote, "You hear, O LORD, the desire of the afflicted; you encourage them, and you listen to their cry" (Ps. 10:17). Yet I also realize that this same writer began his psalm with the question, "Why, O LORD, do you stand far off? Why do you hide yourself in times of trouble?" (Ps. 10:1). The same man who had such great confidence that God would hear his prayer also struggled to understand why his prayers weren't answered sooner and in the way he desired.

That's the way life is on this side of heaven. We are like the man in Mark 9 who asked Jesus *if* he could do anything to help his demon-possessed son. Jesus replied, "If you can? Everything is possible for him who believes." To which the man wisely and immediately exclaimed, "I do believe; help me overcome my unbelief!" (Mark 9:22–24).

Even though it is often difficult for us to pray when we find ourselves in the middle of great trials, that is exactly the time when we most need to pray. Every time we pray, whether it feels like it or not, we are brought into the very throne room of heaven. Jesus himself ushers our prayers into the presence of the Father, and that alone assures us that they will be heard and answered. Prayer is a matter of obedience, but it is also a matter of survival. Prayer is the lifeline of the soul, and we cannot afford to do without it.

So let us pray to the God who hears and answers. Jesus has promised he will see to it that our requests get God's personal attention. But first we must pray. It starts there and nowhere else.

Notes

1. *Who Said It?* (Chicago: Moody Press, 1994), 361.

2. C. S. Lewis, *Christian Reflections* (Grand Rapids: Eerdmans, 1953), 144.

Please, No Empty Rooms

So then, those who suffer according to God's
will should commit themselves to their faithful
Creator and continue to do good.
—1 Peter 4:19

A friend asked me one time to imagine a scene in heaven. Suppose God said, "David, I am about to give you a choice. You know that I am the God who inhabits eternity; time is as nothing to me. I can do with it as I will. But in this one instance, I am going to give you the opportunity to go back in time and relive your life, if you so desire. David, look over there."

As I look over to the spot he indicates, I see scores of people I met through my ordeal with cancer: fellow patients in the hospital, former teammates, amputees now made whole, friends killed by cancer made alive and vigorous once more but now sporting strong and incorruptible bodies.

"David," the Lord continues, "these are the people who were touched in one way or another by your life and your story. Some came to know me through what happened to you. Others were encouraged to stay faithful to me when they saw how you dealt with your own battle against cancer. Still others were motivated by your story to get involved with people who were hurting in order to bring them some measure of relief. They will all bring glory to my name for eternity, and the suffering you bore on earth is partly responsible for putting them here. Now, David, I want you to look over here."

And with that, he shows me another scene, one with far fewer people. I notice that some of the faces I had seen before are now not absent merely from the room but from heaven itself. The few people I see are happy enough, but . . . the room could hold far more than it does. It looks naked, and I do not like it. "Lord," I ask, "what is this place?"

"This is the choice I told you about, David," the Lord responds. "If you wish, I will turn back time and prevent you from getting cancer. You will suffer none of the pain, none of the anguish, none of the awful doubts or anxious moments you endured before. You will go on to a long and successful baseball career, then you will retire and live out your days in luxury and perfect health. You will die at a ripe, old age . . . but the room you see now is what will greet you when you get here. It is your decision; which room do you choose?"

I am glad that this is merely a story and that no such choice awaits me. But even if it did, how could I choose the second room? Knowing what I do now, how could I ever go back to the way I lived before cancer invaded my life? Many people who hear my story think it's a tragedy. I don't feel that way at all.

There is a scene in the movie *Field of Dreams* in which Ray Kinsella tracks down an old ballplayer named "Moonlight" Graham. Graham's career in the major leagues was so short it wasn't even a flash in the pan. He played only a few minutes of one game in the majors, and he never got a chance to bat. That was decades ago. Graham is an old man now. He had become a doctor and had given his life to alleviate what suffering he could in the small town where he lived. They talked about his experiences as a doctor, and then the conversation turned to baseball. Kinsella couldn't get over how short Graham's career had been: "For five minutes you were *that* close to your dream. It would kill some men to be that close to their dream and not to touch it; they'd consider it a tragedy."

Graham looked him in the eye and with a wistful smile said, "Son, if I'd have been a doctor for only five minutes, now *that* would have been a tragedy."

When I look back over the years since my amputation and see all I've learned from other people who have suffered, all I've experienced of other people's love, all God has shown me of his mercy and comfort, all the encouragement my small measure of suffering has given to others, I think, *If I'd have continued on as a ballplayer and missed that, now* that *would have been a tragedy*.

I have learned that God is faithful, even in the midst of cancer. He is faithful, even in the middle of amputation. He is faithful throughout the pain, the suffering, the doubts, the worries, the sleepless nights. When Peter tells us that "those who suffer according to God's will should commit themselves to their faithful Creator and continue to do good," I know it's outstanding advice.

And who suffers "according to God's will"? You do, in some sense at least, if you're a Christian and you're suffering is not "as a murderer or thief or any other kind of criminal, or even as a meddler" (1 Peter 4:15). Suffering comes for all sorts of reasons: We live in a fallen world; we make bad health choices; Satan afflicts us; God wants to use our suffering to glorify him (read John 9 to get a better take on that one). But in the end, if you're a believer, God wants to redeem your suffering and use it for good, somehow. He is a faithful Creator, so we must trust him. We do not yet know how he plans to use our suffering to display his glory before a breathless universe, but we know that's what he's up to. And that's true whether we recover or we don't, whether we live or we die. We just don't know how such a faithful Creator will use our suffering for his glory, but he has said that he will. That is why we must "continue to do good," as long as we're here.

My friend's illustration helps me to put things in perspective. I wouldn't have chosen any of the hardships that befell Jan and me, and I wasn't always the most stellar example of faith while I was enduring them. But God is faithful, and even now I can see how he has chosen to use the difficult circumstances of life for his glory and my benefit. I can honestly say today that I am grateful to have played some small part in it.

But I do have one small request of the Lord. When I get to heaven, I don't want to see any empty rooms. Somehow, that just wouldn't be heaven.

———

Dear Lord,

Sometimes I wish suffering weren't a part of the landscape of life. There is so much uncertainty, so many questions, and so few answers, that at times I do all that I can to avoid suffering. But now I find myself smack dab in the middle of it . . . and there seems to be nowhere to turn, except to you.

I thank you, Lord, that the Bible, your Word, gives such incredible comfort in the midst of storms like this. Help me, Lord, to hold on to those words of encouragement so that I may have the strength I need to endure this journey.

I am so grateful for the many examples in your Word of men and women who have suffered. I am grateful not only for them but also for those who are suffering all around me who yet encourage me not to lose heart. Most important of all to me is that your Son, Jesus, knew suffering more deeply than any of us . . . and yet he did not lose heart. Through his life you have given me the strength to cope in the midst of the storm!

You know, Lord, I'd like to say one more thing before I finish. Thanks for putting the warning sign up there that tells us we will suffer, that suffering is a part of life in this fallen world. But thanks also for allowing us—for allowing me—the freedom to express my fears about the future. For only when I do so am I able to realize my dependence upon the One who understands my suffering better than anyone. Because he did not lose heart when he suffered, I, too, can find the strength to live courageously in my own difficult circumstances.

Amen!

Two
The Pain

"though outwardly we are wasting away"

Throughout my early life and my entire baseball career, I worked on perfecting my body. At one time I had washboard abs, 17-inch biceps, and a 32-inch waist. I worked out daily to keep in shape—but a few years ago an unexpected illness, cancer, came into my life and changed my earthly body forever.

Now as I stand before a mirror, I see quite a different picture. My left arm and shoulder are gone, and it looks as though half my upper body is missing. I have gained over forty pounds since the end of my baseball career, and it is distributed in places it never visited before.

It is obvious to me that our bodies do not last forever. While there is nothing wrong with taking care of our physical bodies—God commands us to care for the vessels that house the Holy Spirit—we must never forget that they are not built to last forever. They *will* fall into increasing disrepair. Therefore we are wise to focus our primary energies not on the strength of our bodies but on that of our spirits. As Paul said, "For physical training is of some value, but godliness has value for all things, holding promise for both the present life and the life to come" (1 Tim. 4:8).

What a Wretched Man I Am!

What a wretched man I am! Who will rescue me from this body of death? Thanks be to God—through Jesus Christ our Lord! So then, I myself in my mind am a slave to God's law, but in the sinful nature a slave to the law of sin.

—Romans 7:24–25

Before I came to faith in Christ, I never thought of myself as a "wretched man," as Paul uses the term in Romans 7. In fact, I thought I was a pretty good guy. I didn't rob banks, I didn't beat up old ladies, I didn't steal cars—I had pretty much avoided all the "biggies." I thought my soul was in great shape.

And when it came to my body? Well, not to brag, but I was quite a specimen. A strong, lean, fighting machine. It's what got me to the major leagues. I thought I was invincible and that nothing would happen to me. "Wretched man?" Not me! My body was in just as good shape as my soul. Maybe better.

When someone believes this kind of thing, as I did, he really can't be too careful about what he reads. The only way to perpetuate such a lie is to keep away from the truth. And to keep away from the truth, you had better avoid the Bible. That was my mistake; I began reading God's Word. And what I found there blew my self-image all to pieces.

I started reading little pieces of good news such as Ecclesiastes 7:20: "There is not a righteous man on earth who does what is right and never sins." I would note verses like Proverbs 20:9: "Who can say, 'I have kept my heart pure; I am clean and without sin'?" I would gulp when I saw that even somebody as "good" as King David could say, "Surely I was sinful at birth, sinful from the time my mother conceived me" (Ps. 51:5). And then the Word started getting personal.

The image I had of myself as a good guy just slightly below the stature of, say, Billy Graham, took a nosedive when I started reading the book of Romans. I soon realized with alarm that I was and am a sinner. "For all have sinned and fall short of the glory of God," Paul wrote in Romans 3:23. I underlined the word *all* in my Bible so I would remember that I qualify, along with everyone else on the planet. That was hard to take, but it would soon get worse. When I got to Romans 6:23, I read that "the wages of sin is death." Now, hold on! I don't rob banks! I don't beat up old ladies! I don't steal cars! Sure, I sin. Everybody does. But . . .

No "buts" about it. "The wages of sin is death." No exceptions. You sin, you die. Period.

I finally realized that because of our sin, all of us already are terminal, whether we have been diagnosed with a terminal illness or not. Fortunately, however, there is more to the message than that. "The wages of sin is death" is only the first half of the verse; the second half says, "but the gift of God is eternal life in Christ Jesus our Lord." And just a little before that Paul had written, "But God demonstrates his own love for us in this: While we were still sinners, Christ died for us" (Rom. 5:8).

This gave me the hope I needed, especially when I read the payoff verse in Romans 8:1: "Therefore, there is now no condemnation for those who are in Christ Jesus." And how did I get "in

Christ Jesus"? What did I have to do? Paul answered my question almost before I could ask it: "If you confess with your mouth, 'Jesus is Lord,' and believe in your heart that God raised him from the dead, you will be saved. For it is with your heart that you believe and are justified, and it is with your mouth that you confess and are saved" (Rom. 10:9–10).

Once I had done that, I was "in Christ." Now my soul truly was in great shape.

And my body? You know the story. When cancer invaded my life, I started to realize very quickly that the "body of death" Paul was talking about didn't refer solely to our souls. I started coming to grips on a very personal level with the magnitude of the fall of man. Like never before, I started to understand the implications of Adam's sin in both the physical and spiritual realms. The curse came home to me: "Cursed is the ground because of you; through painful toil you will eat of it all the days of your life. It will produce thorns and thistles for you, and you will eat the plants of the field. By the sweat of your brow you will eat your food *until you return to the ground, since from it you were taken; for dust you are and to dust you will return*" (Gen. 3:17–19).

Because of sin, both our souls and our bodies were cursed. That is why Paul cries out, "What a wretched man I am!" Wait a minute—me, wretched? You bet. You, wretched? I'm sorry, but the answer is "yes." Then Paul asks his own question—and fortunately for us, gives an answer: "Who will rescue me from this body of death? Thanks be to God—through Jesus Christ our Lord!"

Jesus bore the spiritual penalty for our sin on the cross. That's taken care of the moment we come to him in faith. Yet our physical bodies are still subject to decay. He has promised that one day he will take care of that, too, when he clothes us in indestructible bodies that will never wear out and never feel pain or see decay (see 1 Cor. 15:35–57). But for now, we still see the results of the Fall in our own fragile bodies. We still feel pain. We still suffer. We still watch as disease or accidents or old age cripples, maims, and eventually kills all of us.

Even in this in-between time, however—after our spirit has been renewed but before it's our body's turn—we can look to Jesus Christ and begin to understand how God can provide the comfort, the strength, the encouragement, and the healing that is necessary on the journey of life when we come face-to-face with suffering.

The greatest healing of all occurs when we own up to our sin, confess it, and turn to Jesus in faith. Then his blood washes it all away and transforms us into new creatures, spiritually whole and healed. That is the greatest healing of all, and it prepares us to cope with affliction when it comes barging into our lives.

Thanks be to God—through Jesus Christ our Lord!

We must be made to feel our weakness, our wretchedness, our inability to correct ourselves. We must give up hope in ourselves, and have no hope but in God.[1]

—*Fénelon*

Note

1. Fénelon, *Let Go* (Springdale, Penn.: Whitaker, 1973), 42.

A God for
Fragile Emotions

O LORD, do not rebuke me in your anger or discipline me in
your wrath. Be merciful to me, LORD, for I am faint; O LORD,
heal me, for my bones are in agony. My soul is in anguish. How
long, O LORD, how long? Turn, O LORD, and deliver me; save
me because of your unfailing love. No one remembers you
when he is dead. Who praises you from the grave? I am worn
out from groaning; all night long I flood my bed with weeping
and drench my couch with tears. My eyes grow weak with sorrow; they fail because of all my foes. Away from me, all you
who do evil, for the LORD has heard my weeping. The LORD has
heard my cry for mercy; the LORD accepts my prayer.

—*Psalm 6:1–9*

◆

One thing I love about the Bible is its brutal honesty. It never
shrinks from telling the truth, even if that truth is unlovely
or even downright ugly. And because of that uncompromising honesty, it has the power to set us on a healing track. As Jesus himself
said, "You will know the truth, and the truth will set you free"
(John 8:32).

One of the honest things the Bible tells us is that we are just as
fragile emotionally as we are physically. Some of us don't like to

hear that. It's probably easier for most people to accept physical frailty than it is to admit emotional fragility. I know it was for me.

My strength was never in the physical arena, but in my tough emotional constitution. I considered myself a strong person. I was great at helping everyone else while I suffered with my own pain, privately. I thought I was doing this very well.

In reality, all I was doing was stuffing my pain. I wasn't releasing it to God or to anyone else, and it ate me up from the inside out. I wish that long ago I had read something like the following from Larry Burkett:

> My encouragement to any cancer patient is, do not deceive yourself. Walk in the truth. A positive attitude is always helpful and encouraging, but not when cloaked in denial. Facing mental pain and suffering requires great courage, but in the end, truthfulness and trust in God are the most healthy methods of coping.[1]

In the midst of great physical suffering it is important not to ignore the emotional side of suffering. The advice, "Just suck it up," does not work. Our mental state enormously affects our physical state. Fears, grief, and anger all need to be expressed in order to bring physical healing. When bottled up inside, these emotions will destroy us. God knows what we're feeling anyway, so why try to hide it?

It was so helpful to me during my long bout with depression to read the Psalms. King David, especially, poured out his heart to God. He was absolutely unafraid of bringing all his emotions into the open. Name an emotion, and you can probably find it in one of David's psalms.

Fear? "When I am afraid, I will trust in you" (Ps. 56:3).

Weakness? "Be merciful to me, LORD, for I am faint" (Ps. 6:2).

Anguish? "My soul is in anguish" (Ps. 6:3).

Impatience? "How long, O LORD, how long?" (Ps. 6:3).

Grief? "All night long I flood my bed with weeping and drench my couch with tears" (Ps. 6:6).

Sorrow? "My eyes grow weak with sorrow" (Ps. 6:7).

Note that all of these examples (except for the first one) are from a single psalm! David was unashamed to pour out his heart to God in all its emotional intensity and even fury. And note something else, too: God saw fit to put these emotional Psalms into Holy Scripture. Why? Because he couldn't find anything more doctrinally correct to include and he had to put in something? Hardly. God wants us to be truthful with him, and the Psalms are among the most transparent human records in existence. They prove that it is possible to be both godly and honest.

We are not being honest when we're churning inside and yet go to God in prayer in our best King James vocabulary, trying to sound unperturbed and unruffled and all righteous and holy. That's phony. Whom are we trying to fool, trying to sound so righteous before a holy and all-knowing God? He knows exactly what's going on inside us, even if we won't admit it. In those times we need to follow David's example and tell God exactly how we feel, even though we risk saying "wrong things." God invites us to share our hearts with him, to confess our sins and our fears and our insecurities and our worries, and then to ask him to change our hearts.

Part of gaining emotional health is to admit we're not healthy. We need to accept the fact that we are all emotionally fragile, that we need God and we need others. When I failed to do that, I wound up in depression. When I learned to be honest about my emotions, I discovered a God who had been waiting for me to share my heart.

Don't make the mistake I did. Don't make him wait for you. You can't afford it, and even if you could, why would you want to? That's a costly expense that buys nothing but grief.

Note

1. Larry Burkett, *Damaged But Not Broken* (Chicago: Moody Press, 1996), 116.

Tents Are Temporary

For while we are in this tent, we groan and are burdened,
because we do not wish to be unclothed but to be
clothed with our heavenly dwelling, so that what is mortal may be swallowed up by life. Now it is God who has
made us for this very purpose and has given us the
Spirit as a deposit, guaranteeing what is to come.
—*2 Corinthians 5:4–5*

A tent is a very temporary thing. Of course, no earthly hous-
ing is really permanent—fires, earthquakes, tornadoes, and
wars see to that—but tents are more obviously temporary than
habitations like caves or houses or apartments or even mobile
homes. A tent tears easily, is moved freely, and wears out quickly.

It's no wonder the Bible sees a tent as a good picture of our
bodies.

As one example, consider 2 Peter 1:13–14. Just before he died,
the apostle Peter wrote to some friends to remind them of the
lessons they had learned under his tutelage. He said, "I think it is
right to refresh your memory as long as I live in the tent of this
body, because I know that I will soon put it aside, as our Lord Jesus
Christ has made clear to me."

There's something refreshing about his perspective. Yes, a tent is
temporary, but maybe that's not so bad. If Peter can talk so casually

about "putting it aside," you might suspect that he's looking forward to some other arrangements. It sounds less like he's giving up a home than he is trading in a rental. Which, according to his friend Paul, was exactly what he was doing: "Now we know that if the earthly tent we live in is destroyed, we have a building from God, an eternal house in heaven, not built by human hands" (2 Cor. 5:1).

When you stop to think about it, there are many things about a tent that leave a lot to be desired. They're not the prettiest things in the world. They leak. They're uncomfortable. After a while, they smell. They get moldy. A tent is not made to be a permanent dwelling . . . just as our bodies are not made to be our permanent homes. Now we have a tent; soon we will have a "building," an "eternal house." And did you note the exclusive neighborhood: "in heaven"! No more crummy roadside campgrounds. We won't even have to worry about shoddy carpentry work or a contractor's foul-ups, because our new homes are "not built by human hands."

Thinking about all this brings me great comfort, and if I'm not mistaken, that's the point. God doesn't want us to focus our attention on every rip and tear of the tent because that leads only to discouragement and despair. Yes, we long for freedom from pain and suffering. We long for a time when all things will be perfect. Paul did, too: "Not only so, but we ourselves, who have the first-fruits of the Spirit, groan inwardly as we wait eagerly for our adoption as sons, the redemption of our bodies" (Rom. 8:23).

Our focus, however, must be on the "building" to come, not the "tent" we have now. This is the one message that helped me to get through my ordeal with cancer. In the midst of tremendous fear and doubt and worry, I laid hold of God's promise of a "heavenly dwelling." I took my disintegrating tent and I camped on the deed God had given me for a new home. I knew the Spirit lived within me, and I knew the Bible likens the Spirit to "a deposit, guaranteeing what is to come." As hard as it was to face the very real possibility of my imminent death, this was a great comfort to me.

Speaking of comfort, I'd like to close my thoughts on tents and houses with the following piece, titled "O Mr. Tentmaker." I hope it blesses you as much as it did me.

> It was nice living in this tent when it was strong and secure
>   and the sun was shining and the air was warm.
> But Mr. Tentmaker, it's scary now.
> You see, my tent is acting like it is not going to hold together;
>   the poles seem weak and they shift with the wind.
> A couple of stakes have wiggled loose from the sand;
>   and worst of all, the canvas has a rip.
> It no longer protects me from beating rain or stinging fly.
> It's scary in here, Mr. Tentmaker.
>
> Last week I went to the repair shop and some repairman
>   tried to patch the rip in my canvas.
> It didn't help much, though, because the patch pulled
>   away from
>   the edges and now the tear is worse.
> What troubled me most, Mr. Tentmaker, is that the
>   repairman didn't
>   even seem to notice that I was still in the tent;
>   he just worked on the canvas while I shivered inside.
> I cried out once, but no one heard me.
>
> I guess my first real question is: Why did you give me such a
>   flimsy tent?
> I can see by looking around the campground that some of the
>   tents are
>   much stronger and more stable than mine.
> Why, Mr. Tentmaker, did you pick a tent of such poor quality
>   for me?

And even more important, what do you intend to do about it?

O little tent dweller, as the Creator and Provider of tents,
    I know all about you and your tent, and I love you both.
I made a tent for Myself once, and lived in it on your
        campground.
    My tent was vulnerable, too, and some vicious attackers
        ripped it to pieces
    while I was still in it.
It was a terrible experience, but you will be glad to know they
        couldn't hurt me;
    in fact, the whole occurrence was a tremendous advantage
    because it is this very victory over my enemy that frees me
    to be a present help to you.

O little tent dweller, I am now prepared to come and live in
        your tent with you,
    if you'll invite me.
You'll learn as we dwell together that real security comes from
    my being in your tent with you.
When the storms come, you can huddle in my arms and I'll
        hold you.
When the canvas rips, we'll go to the repair shop together.

Some day, little tent dweller, some day your tent is going to
        collapse;
    you see, I've designed it only for temporary use.
But when it does, you and I are going to leave together.
    I promise not to leave before you do.
And then, free of all that would hinder or restrict,
    we will move to our permanent home and together, forever,
    we will rejoice and be glad.[1]

Someday you will read in the papers that D. L. Moody is dead. Don't you believe a word of it. At that moment I shall have gone up higher; that is all; out of this old clay tenement, into a house that is immortal—a body that death cannot touch, that sin cannot taint; a body fashioned like unto His glorious body. I was born of the flesh in 1837. I was born of the spirit in 1856. That which is born of the flesh may die. That which is born of the spirit will live forever.

—*D. L. Moody*

Notes

1. Anonymous.

Heavenly Physiques

So it will be with the resurrection of the dead. The
body that is sown is perishable, it is raised imperishable; it is sown in dishonor, it is raised in glory; it is
sown in weakness, it is raised in power; it is sown a
natural body, it is raised a spiritual body.
—*1 Corinthians 15:42–44*

In the past week Jan and I learned of two women who underwent mastectomies after year-long battles with cancer. As a result, their husbands walked out on them. Both men were in their early forties, were considered strong Christians, and have become work-out freaks since they abandoned their wives. They live in the gym and exercise for hours every day.

Why did they do it? Was it because their wives' battle for life reminded them of their own mortality? Was it because they couldn't stand the thought of lying next to a surgically altered body? Or was it merely a reflection of a culture that insists on trying to stop time and turn it backward? Just what was it that caused these men to run in the opposite direction from their wedding vows?

I don't know. But I do know our society places gigantic emphasis on making this body look good, while giving no thought whatever to the body that is to come. Maybe these men just fell into that trap. They wouldn't be the first.

Our hope as Christians can never be placed on refurbishing or gussying up our present bodies. You can spend all your time and money on that pursuit if you want to, but in the end you're going to end up looking like the bald man who tries to conceal his shiny scalp with a long wisp of side hair twirled on top of his still-gleaming dome. Nobody is fooled, and you've wasted your efforts.

I don't have time for that nonsense, because I'm getting a brand-new body that comes complete with everything I need. That means a lot to a man who's missing an arm and a shoulder. In the past few years I've met dozens of people who have lost arms or legs or feet or hands. I have come to know many men and women, boys and girls who have been damaged physically, whether through accident, disease, birth defects, or old age. These folks are looking forward to their new bodies every bit as much as I am. They know what it is to be physically limited now, and they can't wait to find out what their new bodies will have to offer.

For me, I've often said that when I get to heaven, I'm looking forward to a new left arm. And for you baseball fans out there, if you think Nolan Ryan threw hard, just wait until I start zinging fastballs toward the *real* home plate!

So what will these new bodies be like? We're given hints in Scripture, but nothing definitive. We do know a few things:

- *They will never decay.* Paul says they will be "imperishable." That means they won't wear out, burn out, or rot out. After you've used your body for a trillion billion years, it will still be as good as new. These bodies won't come with 50,000-mile warranties, because they won't need any warranties at all. Fifty thousand miles or 50,000 light years, the tread on your tires will still be the same.

- *They will never grow ugly.* Paul says they will be "raised in glory." That means that, in heaven, the least attractive resident will have a radiance and beauty that will outshine the sun. There won't be any beauty parlors, because there won't be anything you could do to make any saint the least bit more gorgeous.

- *They will be strong.* Paul says they will be "raised in power." That means there won't be any wheelchairs in heaven. No pneumatic lifts. No crutches, no hospital beds, no braces, no personal trainers. No need to take vitamins A, B, or even C, and you won't ever have to eat spinach if you don't want to.

- *They will be out of this world.* Paul says they will be "spiritual." What exactly is a spiritual body? This one's harder to grasp, since we don't have anything like it on this planet. Paul compares it to a seed. When you plant a seed in the ground, you expect something else to come up. What grows is related to that seed, but it isn't the same as that seed. One writer has said, "An earthly, natural body is fallen and is so temporal, imperfect, and weak. A heavenly, spiritual body will be eternal, perfect and powerful. Like a seed sown in the earth and the plant which proceeds from it, there is continuity but a gloriously evident difference."[1] Like I said—out of this world.

- *They will be like the resurrected body of Jesus.* In Philippians 3:20–21, Paul writes, "But our citizenship is in heaven. And we eagerly await a Savior from there, the Lord Jesus Christ, who, by the power that enables him to bring everything under his control, will transform our lowly bodies so that they will be like his glorious body." This should rock your IQ. If you want to get a hint of what it means to have a body like that of the resurrected Jesus, read the post-resurrection accounts in the Gospels. If your jaw doesn't hit the floor, it must be wired shut.

Folks, I know from experience that this truth has the power to comfort like almost no other. Several years ago when Jan and I were sitting at our dinette table with my father, telling him of my imminent amputation, he sat there and wept. He couldn't believe that part of his son's body soon was going to be cut off. Jan read aloud 1 Corinthians 15:42–44 to give him the assurance that, although I was losing my arm, the day was coming when I would receive a spiritual body that would be raised imperishable, in glory and in power. That text gave my dad hope. It gave him comfort. It helped him to accept what was about to happen to my present body, and it has done the same for me.

I'm looking forward to my new-and-improved heavenly physique. As soon as possible, I plan to take the mound and blow away the first batter I face. And I won't even need any spinach.

Dear Lord,

Being healthy gives me a sense of being invincible—but nothing blows that feeling out of the water more quickly than being faced with some kind of affliction or suffering. Whether I or someone I know is suffering, affliction is a rude awakening to the fact that life is short and each of us is wasting away. Lord, it's times like this that really cause me to think about the things in life that are most important.

During this time of uncertainty, I find myself asking questions I've rarely asked before. After all, there never was a need to ask such questions; I had everything under control. Everything was going great, just as I planned. But now it's so different. I'm scared, and quite frankly, I'm beginning to see a side of me that I don't much like. Suffering does that to a person, I guess.

And yet, as I come to you in all my ugly sinfulness, I now understand what the apostle Paul meant when he said, "What a wretched man I am! Who will rescue me from this body of death? Thanks be to God through Jesus Christ our Lord!" I feel so much like Paul, wretched and wondering who will rescue me. Lord, I now know that if I place my trust in Jesus, it is he who will rescue me from my sin and who will give me the strength to endure this journey of life.

So, where does that leave me? I know this body won't last forever. Yet, Lord, I thank you that even in the midst of living with this broken-down body of mine, you have given me HOPE! Yes, I know that outwardly I am wasting away, but I also know that this pain and suffering have caused me to come face-to-face with my own ugly sinfulness . . . and that you have led me to Jesus, the One who rescues me from this body of death. He provides me with a HOPE that will last forever!

Amen!

Note

1. Walvoord & Zuck, *The Bible Knowledge Commentary* (Wheaton, Ill.: Scripture Press Publications, Victor Books, 1983), 545.

Three
A Renewal

*"yet inwardly we are being
renewed day by day"*

It's a fact of life that the moment we are born, we begin to die. But for the Christian, this is only part of the story (and not even the crucial part). When the Holy Spirit moves into our lives, he begins a massive renovation project on our souls. Day by day he builds into us the Christlike qualities of patience, endurance, kindness, gentleness, goodness, joy, peace.

Perhaps this is why so much of life hurts—the third Person of the Trinity is busy tearing down old walls, pulling up warped floors, yanking out worn cupboards, and putting in new and wear-proof replacements, sent direct from the Manufacturer. He's so good at his work that every "home" he's ever renewed stays in perfect condition for eternity. And you know what? When he's finished, nobody ever misses the old place.

Colorado Winters and Evergreen Grass

For you have been born again, not of perishable seed, but
of imperishable, through the living and enduring word of
God. For, "All men are like grass, and all their glory is
like the flowers of the field; the grass withers and the
flowers fall, but the word of the Lord stands forever."

—1 Peter 1:23–25

As I write this, it's still winter. We're through the worst of it,
but in Colorado where we live, you never know when the
next blizzard is going to come whistling through the mountains.
We can be shooting hoops in 70-degree weather one day and shoveling out our driveway the next. And sometimes the shift can happen in about fifteen minutes!

One thing about winter—it makes you appreciate spring. As I
look out my window, I don't see a lot of flowers. It's hard to spot
much green grass. It wasn't too long ago that we had both, and I
look forward to their return. Now, however, they're either gone
altogether or brown and shriveled. Not the prettiest of pictures but
a very accurate one of life in a fallen world.

Maybe Peter was looking out of a window on a late winter's day
when he wrote his first epistle. Maybe he was staring at a favorite

spot where roses used to bloom and verdant grass once sprouted. Maybe that's what reminded him of something Isaiah had written long before: "All men are like grass, and all their glory is like the flowers of the field; the grass withers and the flowers fall . . ."

No doubt Peter looked at his own body and at the tired forms of those around him and nodded his head that, yes, indeed, the grass does wither and the flowers do fall. That's just the way it is in a fallen world.

Yet this is not only a fallen world, it is also one that has been visited by a redeeming God. And that was Peter's primary focus. He may have considered his battered old body for a while, but he didn't gaze upon it for too long. He wanted to emphasize something else entirely: "For you have been born again, *not* of perishable seed, but of imperishable, through the living and enduring word of God." He recognized the weak and transient nature of physical existence, but he focused on the strong and eternal character of spiritual existence. And what's more, he called attention to the conduit through which that spiritual nature could be piped to frail humanity: the "living and enduring word of God."

It's the Word of God that brings new life to our souls. To see that outwardly we are wasting away, all it takes is a mirror; it takes a different sort of mirror, the Word of God, to show us how to be renewed inwardly, day by day.

God's Word is of enormous importance to both Jan and me, even though in our most difficult times we fed from it in different ways. When I was enduring cancer treatments, it was extremely difficult for me to pick up the Scriptures and read. I didn't want to spend time in God's Word. During that awful time, Jan became my Bible. She was able to share with me what she was learning through her own trials and suffering. She read to me what I wasn't able to read myself. Those practical things helped me stay connected to God's Word and his promises. And through that, I was able to glimpse what he was doing inside me even while an incredibly painful thing was afflicting me physically on the outside.

Jan had her own struggles. There came a time when her emotions hit an all-time low, when her depression bottomed out and she was physically unable to keep up with the demands of our family. One day our kids asked Jan to go with them to the pool, and she just couldn't. She had neither the energy nor the strength. After the kids left and Jan was alone in the house, she shook her fist at God and said, "You know, this really stinks. I can't feel you. I can't see you. I don't see any evidence of you in my life, and I can't sense you. I just ought to turn and run away from you. I ought to turn back to the world. I have enough money. I could go shopping and buy myself anything I want and distract myself. Or I could take up tennis or get into clothing. I ought to turn to the world, because ever since I've been following you, it has gone from bad to worse."

But as she turned to walk away from God, something happened. She realized she couldn't. She knew that the world, for all it has to offer, is temporary. The only thing with eternal value is God and his Word. She knew from experience that his Word is true, so she turned back to him and said, "You know, this really stinks again. Because I cannot run from you, either. So I'm going to trust you. I'm going to believe that you speak the truth in your Word. So please, God, make it good."

And he did! Through his Word, her hope was restored and renewed. Not instantly, but surely.

Our experience has taught Jan and me that God keeps his promises. He is faithful to his Word and it is that Word that he uses to renew us. When our emotions are out of control and we can't feel him or sense him, that is the time we need to rely on the firm foundation of God's Word. His Word sustains us.

A verse in the Psalms captures the heart of our discovery. Psalm 119:92 says, "If your law had not been my delight, I would have perished in my affliction." We can both say a hearty "Amen!" to that. But because we have allowed God's Word to take root in the soil of our souls, we can see it bearing fruit. And the great thing about being born again of imperishable seed is that your flower never falls and your grass never withers.

Not even in a Colorado winter.

———

As Good As Dead

Against all hope, Abraham in hope believed and so became the
father of many nations, just as it had been said to him, "So shall
your offspring be." Without weakening in his faith, he faced the
fact that his body was as good as dead—since he was about a
hundred years old—and that Sarah's womb was also dead. Yet
he did not waver through unbelief regarding the promise of God,
but was strengthened in his faith and gave glory to God, being
fully persuaded that God had power to do what he had promised.

—*Romans 4:18–21*

Most of us don't know for sure whether we really believe in
God's promises until we're as good as dead.

I don't use that phrase, "as good as dead," flippantly. It's an emi-
nently biblical phrase. It's used twice in the New Testament (here
in Romans and in Hebrews 11:12), both times to describe Abraham, the father of Israel and the primary example of faith in both
testaments.

"As good as dead." It doesn't sound very respectful, does it?
Hardly the kind of phrase you'd toss in at a state dinner: "Ladies
and gentlemen, it is my great pleasure to introduce to you Abraham, who is as good as dead."

Maybe it's not one of the most respectful phrases available, but
it is one of the most descriptive. It tells you that things aren't going

so well on the physical side of the ledger. It tells you that the person in question lives on the cusp of eternity. It tells you that the coroner is parked around the corner. And it tells you that if ever there were a time to discover what such a person believes, it's now.

I think that's exactly why Paul uses the phrase in Romans 4 to describe Abraham. The apostle has been arguing that people are saved by faith, not by what they do, and he wants to call Abraham as his star witness. One of the reasons Abraham makes such a good witness is that he is an old man, nearly ready to die. His body doesn't work as it used to (and neither does his wife's). Paul knows that what people really believe often comes out when they're about to die. So he turns to Abraham, the one who is as good as dead, and sees that the old man "did not waver through unbelief regarding the promise of God, but was strengthened in his faith and gave glory to God, being fully persuaded that God had power to do what he had promised."

God, of course, had promised Abraham that he would become the father of many nations, the patriarch of a family whose members would grow as numerous as the stars in the sky. Abraham looked at his ancient, broken-down body, saw it was as good as dead, and replied to the Lord, "Count me in. I believe." In Paul's words, he was "fully persuaded that God had power to do what he had promised."

How about you? Do you have that kind of assurance? Are you "fully persuaded that God has power to do what he has promised"? Even (or especially) when your body is as good as dead?

Recently I have been in contact with Tom Moore, a man who is struggling with a terminal illness. Tom told me that as he lies in bed, unable to do much of anything, he holds on to one fact: When his illness runs its course and his body can hang on no longer, he's going home. He has God's promise of heaven, and that hope sustains him. Tom has a peace that defies the world's expectations because he has taken his stand on the promises of God. Those promises give him the strength to endure whatever time on earth he has left. He is fully persuaded that God has power to do what he has promised. That means a lot, coming from a man who knows he is as good as dead.

Tom and Abraham and many others whose bodies are as good as dead have something else in common, something much more important than the state of their earthly tents. In the words of Hebrews 6:18–19, they have "fled to take hold of the hope offered" to them and have found that hope to be like "an anchor for the soul, firm and secure." As a result of grabbing that anchor, they have been "greatly encouraged"—even when their bodies are as good as dead.

Your body may be in similar shape. And if it isn't now, one day it will be. That's a given in this life. No matter how often we may be miraculously healed or given a new lease on life, someday all of us will look at ourselves in a mirror and see bodies that are "as good as dead." When that day comes, we will be given the ultimate test of what we really believe. Will we pass the test? Or will we fail?

My own body certainly shows signs of wear; my missing left arm and shoulder testify to that every day. Still, by God's grace, it appears as if I'll be around for a while. And in the years that I have left, I want to study for my final test. I find that a text like Psalm 119:28 keeps me focused: "Strengthen me according to your word." And others encourage me right now: "My comfort in my suffering is this; Your promise preserves my life" (Ps. 119:50).

Jan and I have chosen to stand on the promises of God. We stand with Abraham and Tom and men like the great Civil War general Robert E. Lee, who said, "In all my perplexities and distresses, the Bible has never failed to give me light and strength."

We think that's a pretty good place to stand. Because when your body is as good as dead, it's awfully nice to look inside and realize that you are fully persuaded that God has power to do what he has promised.

Superwoman Boxer
No More

But he said to me, "My grace is sufficient for you, for my
power is made perfect in weakness." Therefore I will boast all
the more gladly about my weaknesses, so that Christ's power
may rest on me. That is why, for Christ's sake, I delight in
weaknesses, in insults, in hardships, in persecutions, in difficulties. For when I am weak, then I am strong.
—*2 Corinthians 12:9–10*

If you want to set a world record in the bench press, you don't go
on a diet of bread and water.

If you want to build a skyscraper that can withstand a major
earthquake, you don't build it out of papier-mâché.

If you want a drill bit that can punch holes in diamond, you
don't forge it out of Silly Putty.

So why, if we want to be strong spiritually, does God encourage
us to become weak? What sense does that make?

It makes no sense at all to a world that glories in brute strength.
And because our temporary home is in that world, it often doesn't
make much more sense to us. What does Paul mean in 2 Corinthians 12:9–10? What is he getting at?

Often when I speak, I tell my audience that for many years I
felt as if I were in a prizefight. I thought I had the power to handle

everything. I'd climb into the ring and take one blow after another. Each blow would knock me down, but I would always get up on my own strength. And I'd say, "Look at me, God! Look how strong I am! By my own bootstraps I pulled myself up!" I'd stand tall again, and then POW! Another blow would come:

> my mother's death,
>> my father's death,
>>> Dave's cancer,
>>>> an earthquake,
>>>>> a friend's committing suicide.

After each one of these hits, I'd grab hold of the ropes, pull with all my strength, and stand upright in the ring once more. But the blows kept coming. Finally it seemed as if all I could do was hold on to the ropes . . . and then I felt the Lord prying my fingers loose, one at a time. I remember when it felt as if I were holding on by one finger. I said, "I can't do it anymore! I can't hold on anymore! If one more thing happens, I'm going to lose it."

Then one more thing happened. And I let go.

But when I fell—when I had no more physical or emotional strength left—I was surprised to find that I fell straight into the hands of God. That shocked me. How could this be? I wasn't manipulating circumstances anymore. I wasn't making anything happen. It had to be God who was now making things happen. It had to be God who started bringing people into my life, people who would help me to heal. What a relief to finally realize that it wasn't Jan Dravecky who was in charge, but God!

Paul's words now make more sense to me. He could boast and even delight in his weaknesses because he saw, through suffering, that if anything important was going to get done, it wasn't going to get done by Paul; it would only be accomplished when Paul allowed God to work through him. Paul could make himself as strong as possible, as tough and mean and impregnable as flesh would allow, but any major storm could still snap him in two. An oak tree is strong, but if it gets hit by a two-ton meteorite, the meteorite wins. On the other hand, if God sustains that tree and gives it his own strength, no meteorite is going to budge it, even if the rock is as big as Jupiter.

Don't misunderstand me. God didn't ask Paul to make himself weak, nor does he ask us to do so. That would be unnecessary. You see, what suffering and persecution and pain and difficulties do is not so much *make* us weak, as show us we *are* weak. Without them, we can deceive ourselves into believing we're prizefighters. With them, we're reminded that we're not constructed to function on our own power. As Paul said in another place, "We have this treasure in jars of clay to show that this all-surpassing power is from God and not from us" (2 Cor. 4:7). The trick is to allow suffering to be used as a tool to help us depend on God and not upon ourselves.

One contemporary writer who struggled with cancer wrote, "The view from the valley gave me a focus on Christ that I wouldn't have gained any other way. Stars shine brighter in the desert. There are no obstructions, no distractions, no competing lights. The view from the valley isn't so bad because Jesus shines so clearly."[1]

That is what Paul found, and it is what I found as well. I'm glad I discovered I'm not in the ring alone. I'm glad I don't have to take life's punches all by myself. I'm glad to know I'm weak, but he is strong. And I'm glad I found out that when I fall, I fall straight into his hands. It may not make sense to the world, but what do I care? That's not a fight I have to win. Thank God, my days of super-woman boxing are over.

Note

1. John Wimber, "Signs, Wonders, & Cancer," *Christianity Today* 40, no. 11 (October 7, 1996): 50.

Outside and Inside

... being confident of this, that he who began a
good work in you will carry it on to completion
until the day of Christ Jesus.
—*Philippians 1:6*

... and have put on the new self, which is being renewed
in knowledge in the image of its Creator.
—*Colossians 3:10*

———◆———

Outward and inward. Outside and inside. Very often, the two
have little to do with each other. And it's certainly risky to
make a judgment about one by observing the other.

For example, have you ever bought something to eat based on
the scrumptious pictures gracing its packaging? I have. A few
months ago I bought a low-fat boysenberry sorbet that, judging
from its container, promised to delight my taste buds with its
creamy texture and luscious flavor. Sadly, the only advertising
claim for this confection that proved true was the "low-fat" part.
(In fact, it turned out to be no-fat, since after one taste I banished
it to the back of my freezer until it was thrown out months later.
And if you don't eat it, it's fat-free.)

The same principle holds true for people. Take care that you
don't judge what's happening inside by what you see taking place

outside! Very often the two conditions are heading in opposite directions.

Tracy Keeth used to be quite an athlete. In junior high she played basketball, volleyball, and softball. All that came to an end in high school, however, when Reiter's syndrome (a rare form of arthritis) caused severe pain and swelling in her legs. "I had headaches just from clenching my teeth to fight back the pain," Tracy said. Her condition forced her to spend much of her senior year at home, and in 1992 doctors amputated her right leg. She fought to regain a normal life, but a little more than a year after she lost one leg, doctors were forced to take the other. By this point, if you tried to make a judgment on her "inside" by watching what was happening on her "outside," you'd be making a grave error. In fact, while her body was suffering, her spirit was soaring.

"I haven't been a committed Christian all of my life," Tracy admits. "It's a shame that it takes something like this to bring us closer to God, but that is what happened to me. When I was in so much pain that I couldn't sleep, I spent a great deal of time reading the Bible and in prayer." One night, when the pain was overwhelming, she began thinking how nice it would be to die. But in the same instant she began thinking about the pain Jesus suffered when he was beaten, spit upon, and crucified. And she knew she wanted to know Jesus more intimately than she ever had.

"I have lived life when I really didn't know God," Tracy says, "and I've lived life when I can't get enough of him. I've seen both sides of the fence. Now that I know him, I can't help but smile when I think about what he has done in my life."

What's happened to Tracy has been happening to God's people for centuries. Even as their bodies deteriorate, God is renewing their "new self" in the image of their Creator. While outwardly things look grim, inwardly they're looking brighter all the time.

Heather Grounds is another young woman who has seen how "outside" events don't tell the story of what's happening "inside." When Heather was a senior at Baylor University, her right thigh was diagnosed with synovial sarcoma, a fast-growing cancerous tumor. She left Waco for M. D. Anderson Cancer Center in Houston, where she underwent surgery and began a year of chemotherapy. In all that time, she heard practically nothing from her college friends—a blow that was almost as difficult to take as the cancer. "The ache in my heart from the loss of my friends still remains," she admits. "Yet I have found another friend, the most faithful friend of all—Jesus. I have a deeper reliance on God than I ever had before. He has changed my life so completely that I never want it to be what it was before. The outcome of my sorrow and loss has been sweet because through it the Lord showed me his friendship and closeness."

Heather and Tracy and millions like them are proof positive that God's Spirit often uses hardship to renew us in the image of Christ. What is happening on their "insides" shows us that Paul was right to be so confident that "he who began a good work in you will carry it on to completion until the day of Christ Jesus."

As long as we're alive, that work continues. We look forward to the day, maybe soon, when we will be fully like him, for we shall see him as he is (1 John 3:2). In the meantime, we strive to use our circumstances, whatever they may be, to move us forward inch by inch into greater conformity with the character of Christ. That means, of course, that there's an ever-widening gap between what's on our "outside" and what's on the "inside." But that's OK, as long as what's inside is better than what's advertised on the outside. I'll tell you one thing for certain: I don't want to be a low-fat boysenberry sorbet believer. There's just no market for them.

Dear Lord,

I want to get real honest here. Sometimes it doesn't feel as if I am being renewed inwardly. Quite frankly, it doesn't feel like much of anything—except doubtful, painful, and scary!

Yet I know that the Scripture tells me time and again that you are shaping me, much as the potter shapes his clay. In the midst of all that is happening right now, help me to be moldable. And when I stumble in the process, give me the strength to get back up so that you may continue your work.

It scares me even to pray this prayer because I know it may mean some difficult days are ahead. But Lord, through it all, I really desire to walk more closely with you. There is one thing I ask as you allow me to go through the refining process: Please show yourself to me. Sometimes it gets awfully lonely in the valley of suffering and I need to know you're right by my side. I don't really care how you do it—whether it be through a friend, a word from the Scripture, or straight from you—just do it, please!

I know this prayer may sound as if I'm weak, but the truth of the matter is, I am weak! Lord, I know that it is only by waiting and trusting in you that my strength will be renewed for the journey you have allowed me to walk. As I take these steps, may what is happening on the inside be reflected through my life on the outside so that you may be glorified!

Amen!

Four
Trouble for Now

"For our light and momentary troubles"

We would never make light of the suffering that people endure here on earth. No pain *feels* "light and momentary" while we are in its throes. There is no comparing pain, either; everyone suffers differently and uniquely. What is extremely painful to one person may be no pain at all to another.

But any pain, great or small, *is* momentary in the light of eternity. As Paul wrote, "I consider that our present sufferings are not worth comparing with the glory that will be revealed in us" (Rom. 8:18). There is great comfort in knowing that our suffering will come to an end, that "this too shall pass." And there is even greater comfort in knowing that "glory" awaits. This is the divine trade we make, an exchange of all that we have in return for all that God has. I'm not sure what he gets out of the deal, but it's one I wouldn't dream of turning down.

When Time Stands Still

How long, O LORD? Will you forget me forever? How long will
you hide your face from me? How long must I wrestle with my
thoughts and every day have sorrow in my heart? How long will
my enemy triumph over me? Look on me and answer, O LORD my
God. Give light to my eyes, or I will sleep in death; my enemy will
say, "I have overcome him," and my foes will rejoice when I fall.
But I trust in your unfailing love; my heart rejoices in your salvation. I will sing to the LORD, for he has been good to me.

—*Psalm 13*

Y ou don't have to be Albert Einstein to sense that time is rel-
ative. Anyone who has ever suffered deeply knows how our
sense of time radically changes in periods of acute distress. When
our pain reaches unbearable levels, time seems to stand still; when
at last our suffering gives way to happiness, time seems to thunder
away.

It was that way for both Jan and me when I was fighting my battle against cancer. During those lonely and anxious moments, it
seemed as if all the clocks in the world had forgotten how to move
their hands. And we wondered: How long is this going to last?

Perhaps you're asking that same question right now. While the
Bible calls our troubles "momentary," to us they often seem eternal. "How long is this going to last?" we cry. "O LORD, have you

forgotten me? I can't deal with this any longer! Take me home or restore my health—but no more of this!" For centuries, God's saints have called this kind of prolonged distress "the wilderness."

Psalm 13 is a vivid snapshot of a man of faith stranded in the wilderness. He oscillates between fear and confidence, anger and gratitude, doubt and trust. He's been in the desert a long time—"How long, O LORD?"—and his forced wait has caused him to grow anxious about his future—"Give light to my eyes, or I will sleep in death." He asks four rapid-fire questions, three of which begin with the agonizing phrase, "How long?"

The wilderness will do that to you. It wrings questions out of you like water from a sponge. And like water poured out on a sand dune, those questions get swallowed whole without any answers in return.

The Psalms are a great place to turn when you need a road map through the wilderness. It is somehow encouraging to know that even the great King David, a man after God's own heart, had the same feelings of despair that we do. It somehow lifts our spirits to know that when he was being chased around the literal desert at the point of King Saul's spear, he struggled with his relationship to God. This man whom Scripture calls "the apple of God's eye" sometimes felt like a bowl of rotten fruit.

Although I resonate with David's questions and fears and pleas in the first two-thirds of Psalm 13, I rest in his final two verses: "But I trust in your unfailing love; my heart rejoices in your salvation. I will sing to the LORD, for he has been good to me."

Until this point in his psalm, David poured out everything in his soul to God—and all he found there was sorrow, fear, despair, and anguish. But then it was as if he suddenly realized that no hope was to be found in his shriveled little heart. If hope was to be located, it would have to be sought outside of himself. And that was when he remembered: "He has been good to me." Not *life* has been good to me, or *I* have been good to me, or my *friends* have been good to me. Rather, *he* has been good to me. And that changed everything.

Only when we remember that God has been good to us can we turn from our fears and place our hope in him. He doesn't mind that we pour out our hearts to him; yet when they're empty, he wants us to come to him and be filled.

In the midst of suffering, we may not see any end in sight. The pain may even be intensified because we have no sense of God at a time when we need him the most. In our ministry, we often are forced to watch as a friend's suffering continues, day after day. The situation may go from bad to worse. And then the questions come: Where are you, God? We can't understand. Why don't you do something?

A woman we'll call Sherri came to us months ago after she was diagnosed with cancer. After seven surgeries, doctors amputated her foot and part of her leg. During this crisis one of our staff members, Kim, helped lead Sherri to Christ. A few weeks after the amputation, Sherri's husband walked out on her, taking their children with him. And recently a bone scan came back positive, raising new concerns about whether the cancer has spread into her bones.

Sherri called today, wanting to know where God is in all her troubles. What would you tell her? She's scared and uncertain about her future. She's in the wilderness, and that's a frightening and lonely place to be. I don't know all that Kim told her, but I am quite sure she pointed her to the unfailing love of God, to the salvation he abundantly provides, and to the good things he already has given her. Kim could not promise Sherri that her husband would return or that the cancer wouldn't, but she could plant her feet squarely on the promises of God's unchanging Word and guarantee Sherri that God would never abandon her, that he would never leave her or forsake her.

Grabbing at straws? Hardly. It's more like grabbing an oak tree, like embracing a redwood, like taking hold of Mt. Everest itself.

God may never answer our question "How long?" He may never tell us how much farther we must trudge through the desert. But if our wilderness journey leads us to him, then the road we travel is as surely a highway to heaven as is any more rapid thoroughfare. Who knows when the trip will be over? Maybe tomorrow, maybe next week, or next year. God does not give us an ETA, an Estimated Time of Arrival. But if we belong to him, he does give us a GTA—a Guaranteed Territory of Arrival. And from what we can glimpse in the official travel brochure of his Word, the place is spectacular.

Gold in the Making

In this you greatly rejoice, though now for a little while
you may have had to suffer grief in all kinds of trials.
These have come so that your faith—of greater worth
than gold, which perishes even though refined by fire—
may be proved genuine and may result in praise, glory
and honor when Jesus Christ is revealed.
—1 Peter 1:6–7

The first thing you notice about the refiner's fire is that it's hot. Really hot. Unbearably hot. But that's the only way to get a pure grade of ore.

Dwayne Potteiger can speak from experience about the process. As a teenager, he worked in a foundry just twenty-five feet away from a giant kettle in which iron ore was melted down and refined. Workers would place chunks of crude iron in that kettle, then crank up the furnace to 2,800 degrees. It was so hot that Dwayne felt the heat on his back as he worked. When the molten ore was ready, workers would rake and pull the impurities off the surface, then repeat the procedure until at last only pure iron remained.

In August 1992, Dwayne saw the process again from another, more personal, angle. He was diagnosed with anaplastic astocytoma III, a brain cancer with a survival rate of only three to four years. Suddenly he was in the furnace, and it was hot. Unbearably hot.

Dwayne has three times suffered the pain of a stabilizing halo screwed onto his skull. Radiation treatments leave him exhausted. Chemotherapy made him physically sick, and the steroids he still must take bring horrid side effects. He gets tired of being poked and prodded. The treatments leave him with little strength and endurance; he can only watch as his wife and young daughters deal with their deep emotional pain. And he faces the roller coaster uncertainty of new growths and symptoms.

"These things are the furnace," he says. "I never would have signed up for this, but I wouldn't trade it for anything. God is faithful and God is good. I don't view God's allowing cancer to come into my life as his punishment; I view it as an opportunity to advance the cause of Christ and bring glory to God. The situation itself brings no glory to God, but how I respond to it makes all the difference."

But how can we learn to respond to such fire with such faith? Dwayne has found a phenomenal teacher in 1 Peter 1:6–7. Peter was well acquainted with trials, and experience had taught him that they can best be faced after long reflection on the goodness of God. When he writes, "In *this* you greatly rejoice," he doesn't have in mind his contemporaries' sufferings, but the breathtaking blessings already given them by God. Peter lists at least five of these in the immediately preceding verses:

- A new birth
- A living hope
- An imperishable, divine inheritance
- The shield of God's power
- The completion soon of our salvation

If we meditate on and rejoice in those things, Peter says, the scorching fire of refining can do its crucial work. And what is that work? "That your faith . . . may be proved genuine." Dwayne sees this principle at work in his own life. "What is important is that these trials reveal what's really inside," he says. "What's inside is the gold! This process reveals where my heart really is, what I really believe in."

We, too, have found this to be true. As wrenching as our trials were, they caused us to see that we really did believe what we said we believed. We discovered that we lean on what we truly believe. But that's not all.

When the fire of our battle with cancer and depression grew hotter and hotter, our personal impurities came bubbling to the surface. We were forced to deal with personal issues that, unknowingly, we had hidden for so long. God's refining fire forced us to be real with our friends, with our God, and with each other. When our trials started, it was easy to put up a facade and play the good Christian. But as they progressed—as the fire got ever more intense—it became increasingly difficult to keep what was on the inside from getting outside. Eventually those things did come out—bitterness, fear, lack of self-control, rage, moodiness, doubt—and they weren't pretty (impurities never are; that's why you get rid of them). It was not fun to realize that many of the "Christian" things we did were done for selfish motives. Were we telling people of the love of God primarily for their benefit or for the strokes we would receive in return?

Once we started taking steps to deal with our impurities, however, our faith began to grow. As C. S. Lewis wrote, "If only we have the will to walk, then God is pleased with our stumbles."[1]

How pleased? Peter says that such genuine faith is worth infinitely more than pure gold. He does not merely suggest that genuine faith is *like* gold, that it's somehow the spiritual equivalent of gold; no, he insists faith is far more precious than that. Like gold, faith must be refined through intense heat; but unlike gold, it will not perish when "the heavens will disappear with a roar; the elements will be destroyed by fire, and the earth and everything in it will be laid bare" (2 Peter 3:10). Genuine faith is superior to gold in every way that matters. Gold is a shabby, dull shadow of the reality that is genuine faith. Even the purest gold will one day perish, but genuine faith gives birth to eternal praise, glory, and honor.

Sure, being in the fire hurts. We won't lie about that, and neither does God. Yet what he's after is genuine faith, and the only way to purify that kind of precious ore is through the application of intense heat.

We'll let Dwayne have the last word. "The journey I am on adds an incredible authenticity to the message of the Cross," he says. "I have gained confidence in God's undergirding presence with us. In the midst of my uncertain circumstances, I can testify to God's goodness. My mortality is in front of me. I speak as a dying man to a dying people. And that makes a tremendous difference."

Affliction is gold in the making for the child of God
and God is the one who holds the timepiece.

—*Ron Lee Davis*

Notes

1. C. S. Lewis, *Screwtape Letters*, Ch. 8

No One Will Take
Away Your Joy

I tell you the truth, you will weep and mourn while the world
rejoices. You will grieve, but your grief will turn to joy. A
woman giving birth to a child has pain because her time has
come; but when her baby is born she forgets the anguish
because of her joy that a child is born into the world. So with
you: Now is your time of grief, but I will see you again and
you will rejoice, and no one will take away your joy.

—John 16:20–22

Could anyone live in a world without hope?
Could you?

Just imagine, if you dare, what such a horrible world would be
like:

- Never would you hear someone say, "I'm looking forward to
  ..." or "I can't wait until ..." or "Every cloud has a silver lin-
  ing." In such a world there would be nothing to look forward
  to, no happy event to anticipate, no storm that ever died away.
- No one would ever go to sleep expecting a better day tomorrow. No one would ever get up on the right side of the bed.
  No calendars would ever circle a "red letter day," for there
  wouldn't be any.

- Never would visitors leave a hospital, a school, a rest home, or even a church with more optimism than what they brought in.

Hope is perhaps the most precious commodity we have. Hope has the power to splash living colors on bleak and barren landscapes, to fill empty chests with golden treasures, and to infuse life and vitality where before there was only death and despair.

Jesus knew well the awesome power of hope, and that is why he poured an ocean of it on his disciples shortly before he was taken away to be crucified. And yet how honestly he poured! Who among us would begin a warm bath of hope with a bracing shower of reality? Yet that is just what the Master did. Before he lavished on his men this gift of hope, he declared to them why they would need it so badly. "I tell you the truth," he said, "you will weep and mourn . . . you will grieve."

Jesus is always candid with his followers, both then and now. He knows the end from the beginning and is aware that the middle is often filled with pain, tears, and grief. "You *will* weep and mourn," he tells his men (and us). "You *will* grieve."

And yet that is not the whole story! For the world Jesus created is decidedly *not* a world without hope. In fact, it's fairly crammed with the stuff! Jesus knew the anguish that was about to engulf his disciples. He knew the torrents of grief that would rock them when, in just a little while, wicked hands would nail their Glory to a cross. But he also knew that no grave of granite could long entomb that Glory. That is why he also told them, "Your grief will turn to joy. . . . I will see you again and you will rejoice, *and no one will take away your joy.*"

Don't miss that last, glorious promise! *No one will take away your joy.*

But, Lord! Aren't imprisonments in store for your disciples?

No one will take away your joy.

Aren't savage beatings just around the corner?

No one will take away your joy.

Won't your men be mocked? Ridiculed? Scorned? And won't they finally be tortured and killed?

No one will take away your joy.

Jesus knew everything that was coming. And yet he had the audacity—or was it the authority?—to say, *no one will take away your joy.*

And now for the really good news: His promise belongs as much to you as it did to the eleven! Why? Because he based it on a single, priceless fact: "I will see you again." Do you share that conviction? Then so will you share the promise. As surely as one day the Lord will greet each of his children, so surely will he immerse us in his joy—a joy that no one will take away.

But, Lord, I'm in such pain!

No one will take away your joy.

But the doctors have given up hope!

No one will take away your joy.

But my whole world feels like it's caving in!

No one will take away your joy.

That is our hope. That is the glorious hope promised us. And that is the hope that is able to see us through all of our tears, all of our groans, and all of our grief.

It's as certain as the promise of Jesus.

————

There is a sweet joy which comes to us through sorrow.[1]

—*Charles Haddon Spurgeon*

Note

1. *Who Said It?* (Chicago: Moody Press, 1994), 407.

Buoyant to the End

I consider that our present sufferings are not worth comparing with the glory that will be revealed in us.

—*Romans 8:18*

Carolyn Wilson is far more familiar with heartache than any of us would ever wish to be. Countless nights she has soaked her pillow with tears, and innumerable days her eyes have grown red from weeping. Yet through it all, the truth of Romans 8:18 sustains her. Through it all, she can confidently say, "It's worth it all."

How is this possible?

That's a crucial question, but before we can understand the "how," we must get some idea of the "what." And believe me, the "what" isn't pretty. Carolyn has a deep understanding of what Paul means when he talks about "our present sufferings."

For many years, Carolyn endured the pain and loneliness of a dysfunctional marriage for her children's sake. When Carolyn's oldest daughter, Susan, was seventeen, doctors diagnosed her with Hodgkin's lymphoma. Now the pain of an empty marriage was multiplied by the threat of cancer. Two years later, the twenty-two-year marriage disintegrated under the strain.

Yet the tears would continue. Just seven years after the breakup, Carolyn's younger daughter, Keri, was diagnosed with desmoid tumors on one thigh. Radical surgery removed the tumors without resorting to amputation, but in recent days several tumors have reappeared and doctors are scrambling to try new treatments. As of this writing, Keri's prognosis is unclear.

And yet Carolyn clings to the truth of Romans 8:18. She says, "God does not waste our tears or sorrows. I have always believed that he gathers my tears into a bottle and that one day each tear will be a jewel in eternity. I believe this because he says he will redeem them all. He will turn my mourning into dancing and my sorrows into joy. It doesn't make it easy, but this sure makes it bearable."

Those who think Carolyn's words reflect nothing but wishful thinking are simply wrong. Already she has seen God redeem some of her pain, and she takes that small redemption as a "down payment" on what is to come. Remember Susan? She is now thirty years of age, married, has a son, and is working with us at the Outreach of Hope. "God already has redeemed Susan's suffering," Carolyn says. "I believe he prepared her for the ministry she is doing at the Outreach of Hope. She is able to help others because she understands their pain."

When terrible pain comes into our lives, we are often tempted to give in to the idea that Romans 8:18 is little more than wishful thinking. Never fall for this devilish trap! Remember that the writer of this verse was no dreamy-eyed idealist. No, Paul was the consummate realist. Yet his reality was not confined to the fishbowl of earthly existence but encompassed the vast, unsearchable reaches of heaven. Paul never downplayed the jagged pain of life here below, he simply emphasized the infinitely greater rewards of life above. Paul would never think of telling someone, "Oh, please, grow up. Your pain is not so bad!" He would be more likely to say, "Oh, please, *look* up! The glory that awaits you is worth it all!"

Such a conviction takes on even greater weight when you consider that Paul penned these words around A.D. 57, at least two years *after* he wrote 1 and 2 Corinthians, in which he sketched out some of his own sufferings:

> To this very hour we go hungry and thirsty, we are in rags, we are brutally treated, we are homeless. . . . Up to this moment we have become the scum of the earth, the refuse of the world (1 Cor. 4:11, 13).

> I have worked much harder, been in prison more frequently, been flogged more severely, and been exposed to death again and again. Five times I received from the Jews the forty lashes minus one. Three times I was beaten with rods, once I was stoned, three times I was shipwrecked, I spent a night and a day in the open sea, I have been constantly on the move. I have been in danger from rivers, in danger from bandits, in danger from my own countrymen, in danger from Gentiles; in danger in the city, in danger in the country, in danger at sea; and in danger from false brothers. I have labored and toiled and have often gone without sleep; I have known hunger and thirst and have often gone without food; I have been cold and naked. Besides everything else, I face daily the pressure of my concern for all the churches (2 Cor. 11:23–28).

This man knew all about sufferings. He never minimized them, never hid from them, and never shrank from them. Yet neither did he allow them to take his focus off a bigger truth, that his God would one day soon heap upon him blessings infinitely greater than the very real hardships he faced while living on this planet. It was that glorious truth that not only kept him going but that kept him hopeful and buoyant and irrepressible to the end. It has done the same for Carolyn Wilson.

And it can do the same for you . . . if you'll just let it do the mighty work God designed for it to accomplish.

———

Dear Lord,

It is so hard for me to see my suffering as light and momentary. I feel as if the walls are crashing in on all sides and there is no relief in sight. I not only feel this way about myself, but when I look at the world around me and see all the horrible things happening to others, I wonder, is this "light" and "momentary"? Often I get confused and struggle in trying to make sense of it all.

Ah! But then I look into your Word and see that no one could have suffered more deeply than those who are described in the Bible. Men and women were slaughtered because they believed in Jesus. Then I observe how much Jesus suffered on my behalf . . . and I begin to see that my suffering doesn't begin to compare to what he endured for me.

Lord, not only do I see this in your Word, but I also see it in those around me who are suffering. Thank you for the encouragement you have given me through their lives. In the midst of our light and momentary troubles, I am slowly beginning to realize that I am gold in the making.

I have to say just one thing, though. When I am overwhelmed by the suffering, I'm so grateful that you don't sit on your throne, shaking your finger at me in disgust because I'm not handling it well. No, you chose to come off your throne to embrace me and show me through Jesus, through healing words of Scripture, and through loving friends, that you really do care for me. Compared with what awaits us on the other side, I guess these really are just light and momentary troubles. Thanks for helping me to see that more clearly.

Amen!

———

Five
What Good Is Our Suffering?

*"are achieving for us an eternal glory
that far outweighs them all"*

What is "glory"? Glory is what you see when you peer out of an airplane at 30,000 feet and are swept away by the bright glow of an orange and pink and red and purple sunset flaming its brilliance behind the snow-capped peaks of a majestic mountain range. Glory is beauty. Glory is splendor. Glory is magnificence. Glory is all that is worthy of praise and honor and shouts of great joy.

And it is glory that our Father in heaven plans to shower upon us in downpours that will never cease. But not now. Not quite yet. As Robert C. McQuilken has said, "It is suffering and then glory. Not to have the suffering means not to have the glory."

No Contradiction

And we rejoice in the hope of the glory of God. Not only so,
but we also rejoice in our sufferings, because we know that
suffering produces perseverance; perseverance, character;
and character, hope. And hope does not disappoint us,
because God has poured out his love into our hearts
by the Holy Spirit, whom he has given us.

—Romans 5:2–5

Some things just don't seem to go together: oil and water, asparagus and ice cream, gasoline and blow torches, icebergs and iguanas. They just don't mix; they're incompatible, just like joy and suffering. Right?

Well, not exactly.

As hard as it is for us to understand (let alone experience), Scripture often pairs these two seeming opposites. Ponder just a few examples:

- "Consider it pure joy, my brothers, whenever you face trials of many kinds" (James 1:2).
- "If you should suffer for what is right, you are blessed" (1 Peter 3:14).
- "Rejoice that you participate in the sufferings of Christ" (1 Peter 4:13).
- "I rejoice in what was suffered for you" (Col. 1:24).
- "Sorrowful, yet always rejoicing" (2 Cor. 6:10).

When such a puzzling combination appears so often in Scripture, we ought to stop a moment and try to make sense of it. What are we to make of this odd pairing? Is the true patron saint of Christianity really the Marquis de Sade? Are we *really* to rejoice in our trials? And if so, how?

First, it's important to see that Scripture never glorifies suffering for its own sake. The kind of suffering the Bible so consistently pairs with joy is not pain for pain's sake, but suffering that produces something else, suffering that goes somewhere, suffering that creates godly qualities in us that gladden the heart of God.

The apostle Paul makes this clear in Romans 5:3 when he writes, "We also rejoice in our sufferings, *because we know that suffering produces perseverance.*" He does not say, "We rejoice in our sufferings, because excruciating pain is its own reward." We can rejoice in our trials because we know that, when properly cultivated, they will blossom into precious, divine fruit.

But here we must be careful. Few things make Jan and me angrier than reality-denying speeches that go something like this: "Oh, praise the Lord I'm going through this! Praise the Lord for this pain!" That may sound spiritual, but it's not. It's false. Suffering is not a pleasant thing, and to limp around with a fake smile on our lips and saccharine words on our tongue does a terrible disservice to the gospel. If pain itself were so great, why is God going to do away with it in heaven? No, it's not the pain for which we are to be joyful, but the good results that it can produce in us. To deny the pain and the suffering and the agony is to lie and to cease living in the truth. And that neither honors God nor helps us.

And still we are to "rejoice in our sufferings." The word Paul uses for "rejoice" here might better be translated as "glory" or even "exult." He does not mean that our sufferings should naturally make us happy, but that we must choose to glory in them *because* "suffering produces perseverance; perseverance, character; and character, hope." If we begin by putting our hope in God (5:2), Paul insists, then even our sufferings can themselves lead to greater hope (5:4)—surely not a vicious circle but an invigorating and welcome one.

And yet ... does this really work? Can life really turn out like this, or is this pairing of suffering and joy just a bad joke?

In his old-but-still-lively commentary on Romans, William R. Newell briefly tells the story of "Mary," a Christian suffering under Communist rule in northern Siberia. Newell reproduces part of a letter Mary somehow got to the West:

> The best thing to report is, that I feel so happy here. It would be so easy to grow bitter if one lost the spiritual viewpoint and began to look at circumstances. I am learning to thank God for literally everything that comes. I experienced so many things that looked terrible, but which finally brought me closer to Him. Each time circumstances became lighter, I was tempted to break fellowship with the Lord. How can I do otherwise than thank Him for additional hardships? They only help me to what I always longed for— a continuous, unbroken abiding in Him. Every so-called hard experience is just another step higher and closer to Him.[1]

Did you notice? Mary was not enthused about the sufferings themselves, but about what they were doing in her. This is exactly Paul's message in Romans 5:2–5. Mary exulted in her sufferings because they took her "another step higher and closer to Him"— another step closer to her Fountain of Hope. Newell also tells us of a friend of Mary's, a new convert who discovered this same unworldly dynamic at work in her own life. "Barbara" was imprisoned after she publicly declared her faith in Christ, and Mary feared the worst. But this was the result:

> Yesterday, for the first time, I saw our dear Barbara in prison. She looked very thin, pale, and with marks of beatings. The only bright thing about her were her eyes, bright and filled with heavenly peace and even joy. How happy are those who have it! It comes through suffering. Hence we must not be afraid of any sufferings or privations. I asked her, through the bars, "Barbara, are you not sorry for what you have done?" "No," she firmly responded. "If they would free me, I would go again and tell my comrades about the marvelous love of Christ. I am very glad that the Lord loves me so much and counts me worthy to suffer for Him."[2]

Probably we are not suffering for of our faith in a hostile Communist land. Our suffering is more likely due to a body gone awry. Yet the principle is exactly the same in both cases. We can rejoice, even exult, in our sufferings *because they bring us another step higher and closer to our Hope, Jesus Christ*. As Nicholas Wolterstorff has written in his poignant *Lament for a Son*, "In the valley of suffering, despair and bitterness are brewed. But there also character is made. The valley of suffering is the vale of soul-making."[3]

And in such a vale, we really can rejoice without the slightest contradiction.

Notes

1. William R. Newell, *Romans Verse by Verse* (Chicago: Grace Publications, 1945), 167–68.

2. Ibid., 168.

3. Nicholas Wolterstorff, *Lament for a Son* (Grand Rapids: Eerdmans, 1987), 97.

After All, I'm an Heir

Now if we are children, then we are heirs—heirs of
God and co-heirs with Christ, if indeed we share in his
sufferings in order that we may also share in his glory.

—*Romans 8:17*

There may be a lot of ways to become wealthy in this world, but one of the easiest methods is to be named an heir. Even if you don't know what you did to become one.

In late 1996 a Spanish businessman, Eduardo Sierra, was away on business in Stockholm, Sweden. While there, he decided to visit a nearby church to pray. The building was empty except for a coffin containing the remains of a recently deceased man. Eduardo knelt and prayed for the deceased, then signed a condolence book after he saw a note requesting that all who prayed for the dead man also sign their names and addresses. Eduardo noted with sadness that his was the first name on the list.

Several weeks passed and Eduardo nearly forgot about the prayer he had offered on behalf of a man he had never met. So he was surprised one day to get a call from the Swedish capital from another man who also was unknown to him. The man was an attorney and the conversation went something like this:

"Mr. Sierra, perhaps you remember saying a prayer several weeks ago in Stockholm for the recently deceased Mr. Jens Svenson. Mr. Svenson was a seventy-three-year-old real estate dealer with no close relatives. He had stipulated in his will that 'whoever prays for my soul gets all my belongings.' Since you were the only person who signed the condolence book, all of Mr. Svenson's assets, in the amount of more than $1 million, are now legally yours. How would you like to arrange for transfer of these funds."[1]

In the blink of an eye, Eduardo Sierra had become a very wealthy man. He had never met Jens Svenson—he had only read of him— but suddenly everything that once belonged to Mr. Svenson now belonged to Eduardo. That's what it can mean to be an heir.

That story floored me when I first heard it. No matter what you think about the legitimacy of praying for the souls of the deceased, it's almost impossible not to put yourself in Eduardo's shoes, isn't it? You almost can't help but wonder what it would feel like to be Eduardo and suddenly find yourself the heir of an enormous fortune. You know your prayer didn't "earn" you the windfall; rather, everything depended on the grace of the one who named you heir.

I wonder—if a story like this can stoke our imaginations, why doesn't a text like Romans 8:17 fire it all the more? It's true that Eduardo inherited more than a million dollars, but a single poor investment could make all that money disappear. Or it could be stolen. Embezzled. Lost. And even if it multiplies itself ten times in the next few years, one day it will be Eduardo's turn to die, and he won't be able to take the cash with him any more than Mr. Svenson could.

On the other hand, the inheritance promised to believers can never be stolen, embezzled, lost, or otherwise taken away. It's eternal. And it isn't merely a million bucks—it's everything God has. This universe is vast, and whatever's out there—a solar system of gold? a constellation of sapphires? a galaxy of diamonds?—belongs to God. And he has promised to give it all to his heirs! If you're a believer, that means you.

There's more than that, however. Much more. As vast as the cosmos is, it's only a tiny fraction of God's estate. The riches of God can't begin to be contained in something as puny as this universe. And you have been named God's heir! That means that whatever he has, you will have.

Who can wrap their mind around that?

One word of caution, however. Whenever you find yourself named as an heir, you'd be wise to check the will carefully. Every word counts. That is certainly true with Romans 8:17. Read it again, slowly. First the declaration: "Now if we are children, then we are heirs—heirs of God and co-heirs with Christ. . . ." Are you a child of God through faith in Christ? If you can answer "Yes!" then this text declares you an heir of God. Astonishing! Fabulous! Unbelievable! True enough—but keep reading: "*if* indeed we share in his sufferings in order that we may also share in his glory."

What power tiny words can contain!

If we share in Christ's sufferings, Paul insists, only then will we share in his glory. If we want the glory, then we must expect the suffering. One doesn't come without the other. Paul can't conceive of a Christian who goes through this life without suffering. That is why he could write in Philippians 1:29, "For it has been granted to you on behalf of Christ not only to believe on him, *but also to suffer for him.*" The word translated "granted" in this verse is a verbal form of a Greek word usually rendered "grace." We have been graced, Paul says, not only with the faith that brings us into God's family (something we all cherish) but also with the suffering that inevitably accompanies that faith (a gift we'd just as soon leave unopened). The faith and the suffering are equally a gift of God's grace. And together they work to make us heirs of the Lord of glory.

We may never know all the reasons why suffering should play such a big role in the drama God is directing on this planet. Yet when we read his Word—when we check the script and peruse the will—we can clearly see that the play doesn't go on without it. We may not understand this, but it's true. The blockbuster little word *if* sees to that. *If* we share in his sufferings, *then* we will also share in his glory. How do we respond to such news?

I don't know about you, but when the promise is that huge and the promise Giver is that faithful, I can live with a little ambiguity.

After all, I'm an heir, you know.

Note

1. Wire reports (October 1996).

See You at the Ceremony

"Behold, I am coming soon! My reward is with me, and I
will give to everyone according to what he has done."
—*Revelation 22:12*

It's a no-brainer that your past affects your present. And it's obvious that your present affects your future. But do you ever stop to ponder how your future affects your present?

Don't get the wrong idea. I'm not talking about some brain-exploding science fiction tale where somebody travels back in time to become his own great-grandfather. That kind of stuff might be fun to ponder for a while, but it has nothing to do with reality (although, come to think of it, when I look at pictures of my great-grandfather . . .).

What I have in mind is something far more potent, far more down-to-earth than the fancies of science fiction. God's Word tells us that pondering our future ought to have a profound effect on the way we live in the present, *especially* when life's trials tempt us to give up hope and toss in the towel. God takes great pains to remind us that he delights in rewarding his children for lives lived well . And he especially wants us to remember this when life doesn't seem either fair or good.

That's why the Lord talks about rewards so often. He wants us to know that the day is coming soon when he will reach into the inexhaustible treasure chest of heaven and pour the most precious and exotic rewards imaginable (though they're really past imagining) on the heads of his faithful children. That day is as real and as tangible to him now as this moment is to us. And that is why he urges us, pleads with us, even begs us to keep going, even if we feel we can't move another step.

"Do not throw away your confidence," pleads the writer of Hebrews to a congregation soaked in suffering. "It will be richly rewarded. You need to persevere so that when you have done the will of God, you will receive what he has promised" (Heb. 10:35–36).

That's a potent promise. But somehow, we adults often miss its power. Kids seem to have a natural understanding that if a person they know to be faithful makes a promise—especially a big promise—it's worth sticking with the program, however nerve-racking the wait. But as our birthdays mount, sometimes the power of promises peters out. It's too bad. Way too bad. Joni Eareckson Tada writes:

> Maybe some adults pooh-pooh the idea of rewards, but I don't. The child in me jumps up and down to think God might actually reward me something. I remember when I took piano lessons as a kid and would squirm with delight on my bench whenever Mrs. Merson pasted gold crowns on my sheet music for a job well done. I wasn't so much overjoyed with my performance as I was in pleasing Mrs. Merson. My focus wasn't on what I did; it was on her approval. Sophisticated adults aren't into such whimsy, but children sure are.[1]

I think Joni's right on target here. But what she writes next is even more gripping. Joni, you probably know, is a quadriplegic whose ministry, Joni & Friends, reaches out across the world to encourage people with severe physical handicaps. Sitting in her wheelchair, Joni has thought a lot about heaven, and a big part of her heavenly meditations center on the rewards God says he's anxious to give her. That thought alone gets Joni jumping up and down, at least in spirit. She says:

> Nothing is so obvious in a heavenly minded child of God as his undisguised pleasure in receiving a reward—a reward that reflects the approval of the Father. C. S. Lewis said, "To please God . . . to be a real ingredient in the divine happiness . . . to be loved by God, not merely pitied, but delighted in as an artist delights in his work or a father in a son—it seems impossible, a weight or burden of glory which our thoughts can hardly sustain. But so it is."
>
> So, for all the children whom Jesus said were best fit for the kingdom of heaven, get ready for God to show you not only His pleasure, but His approval.[2]

This is how God intends for the future to change our present. Not through science fiction whimsy but through prophetic fact as declared by the God "who inhabits eternity." God plans to reward us one day according to how we live today. And he wants this knowledge to transform our day-to-day journey. The apostle Paul made this clear when he wrote, "For we must all appear before the judgment seat of Christ, that each one may receive what is due him for the things done while in the body, whether good or bad" (2 Cor. 5:10).

That "good or bad" stuff sends shivers down the spines of some Christians, but it isn't meant to. Paul does not intend to scare people but to excite them. He wants to fill them with holy longing, not with awful dread. Of course, there is a real danger that any one of us could be found on the "bad" side of the ledger rather than the "good." But it isn't necessary, and it isn't what God wants. That's why he repeats his message so often:

> "Therefore judge nothing before the appointed time; wait till the Lord comes. He will bring to light what is hidden in

darkness and will expose the motives of men's hearts. At that time each will receive his praise from God" (1 Cor. 4:5).

"Serve wholeheartedly, as if you were serving the Lord, not men, because you know that the Lord will reward everyone for whatever good he does, whether he is slave or free" (Eph. 6:7–8).

"Whatever you do, work at it with all your heart, as working for the Lord, not for men, since you know that you will receive an inheritance from the Lord as a reward" (Col. 3:23–24).

Never forget that God has a reward with your name on it, and all you have to do to receive it is to remain faithful and hang in there. Don't give up. It may seem like a long road ahead, but from the Bible's viewpoint, "in just a very little while, 'He who is coming will come and will not delay'" (Heb. 10:37). And what will he do when he comes? I'll let him tell you himself:

"Behold, I am coming soon! My reward is with me, and I will give to everyone according to what he has done."

So do well. Hang in there. Don't lose hope. And I'll see you at the rewards ceremony.

Notes

1. Joni Eareckson Tada, *Heaven: Your Real Home* (Grand Rapids: Zondervan, 1985), 56.
2. Ibid.

Minor League Thinking, Major League Benefits

Praise be to the God and Father of our Lord Jesus
Christ! In his great mercy he has given us new birth into
a living hope through the resurrection of Jesus Christ
from the dead, and into an inheritance that can never
perish, spoil or fade—kept in heaven for you.
—*1 Peter 1:3–4*

When you're playing baseball in the minor leagues, you'd better learn to like buses. Because whether you like it or not, you're going to be seeing a lot of them.

That's because minor leaguers don't generally fly to their games in jet airliners as do their major league counterparts. The money just isn't there. If a minor league ballplayer is lucky, his club owns a nice, air-conditioned bus with comfortable reclining seats and tinted windows to keep out the sun's glare. If he's not so lucky, he might have to get used to riding on air shocks (air shocks, because the metal ones fell off and there's nothing left but air) and torn vinyl seats that stick to you like Velcro.

But either way, in a sleek new bus or a crummy old one, the trips from ballpark to ballpark can get long. If you don't know how to play solitaire when you get drafted, you learn by the time you discover the Mudhens play in Toledo. Minor leaguers spend hundreds of hours in cramped, moving quarters, trying to get from national anthem to national anthem. No matter how long the trip may be, however, they can count on one thing: The length of their journey never alters the reality of their destination. Whether it takes two hours, four hours, or ten hours (with a couple of flat tires), he knows he'll get there eventually. Toledo was still there, last time he checked.

I think it's time we apply some of this minor league thinking to the real major league. And I'm not talking about baseball. I'm talking about the only league that ultimately counts—the one where God is the owner, founder, and commissioner, where the stadium is paved with transparent gold, and where all the players are known as the saints. I'm talking about eternity.

A little minor league thinking could help us in a major way. Sometimes we're tempted to think that life's hardships and setbacks and pain and loss have somehow managed to wipe eternity off the map. We imagine that our suffering demonstrates there is no such place as heaven and there is no end to the pain. When thoughts like that begin to bedevil us, we need a dose of minor league thinking. Every minor leaguer knows that, no matter how bumpy and uncomfortable and long the trip to the next ballfield might be, *the length of the journey never alters the reality of his destination.* The trip won't last forever and the diamond will be waiting for him at the end.

In the same way, the Bible promises us that no matter how difficult our journey may become, *the length of our journey never alters the reality of our destination.* That's what Peter meant when he declared that all those who have been given "new birth into a living hope through the resurrection of Jesus Christ from the dead" are also guaranteed "an inheritance that can never perish, spoil or fade." And why is that inheritance so secure? Because it is "kept in heaven for you."

This is simply Peter's way of telling us that the length of our journey never alters the reality of our destination. We might be riding in a dilapidated, broken-down old wreck of a bus. We might be several hundred miles from our destination, with two flat tires behind us and a bald spare in front of us. We might be hot, tired, and discouraged, but if we can remember the minor leaguer's creed, we'll be all right: *The length of the journey never alters the reality of our destination.* Our inheritance will be right there in heaven, waiting for us, whenever we arrive—perfect, imperishable, unspoiled, vibrant, and oh, so real.

It was this truth that kept Jan going in the midst of her depression. She learned that nothing is secure but eternal life. Everything else passes. Great comfort and even joy came to her when she focused on the fact that nothing could take this away from her. Even when she was suffering great emotional trauma and felt as if she were losing her mind, she found great comfort in John 10:27–29 where Jesus said, "My sheep listen to my voice; I know them, and they follow me. I give them eternal life, and they shall never perish; no one can snatch them out of my hand. My Father, who has given them to me, is greater than all; no one can snatch them out of my Father's hand." And when she paired this with Romans 8:38–39—"For I am convinced that neither death nor life, neither angels nor demons, neither the present nor the future, nor any powers, neither height nor depth, nor anything else in all creation, will be able to separate us from the love of God that is in Christ Jesus our Lord"—the effect was incalculably powerful. She had seen that God was faithful to his many other promises; she would trust him again with this one.

That's minor league thinking that results in major league benefits. The point of the trip is to arrive at the destination. No one claims that the long hours spent in a creaky, battered old bus will always be pleasant; what is certain is that the ballpark awaits, freshly groomed and ready to welcome the saints who belong there.

I think Peter must have been a ballplayer at one time. At least, he sure had this minor league creed down pat. I'll bet he's a southpaw—it sounds like something a lefty might say: *The length of our journey never alters the reality of our destination.*

I like the sound of that. Better yet, I like its truth. And no Greyhound on the face of the earth can change it one iota (tinted windows or not).

———

Dear Lord,

When I began reading this book, I didn't know that there would be some very hard things to deal with. The fact that suffering is a part of life, period, was tough enough—but then to have to face the reality that I am wasting away . . . well, all I can say, Lord, is that this hasn't been a cakewalk.

Yet now you have brought me to a place of genuine HOPE! My suffering is producing something in me that far outweighs all I am going through. This is something to rejoice about, even in the midst of the battle.

As I read about people such as Lew Gilbert, Lord, I can't help but be encouraged. Here's a man who has been diagnosed with cancer, and to hear him say he's the happiest he's been in sixty-one years of life—well, it's absolutely incredible. Knowing that good is being accomplished through the suffering, even though there are times I certainly don't feel it, just blows me away.

I am amazed at how you work. I may not fully understand, but I am left with only one thing to do: I thank you for whatever you are doing in my life. Although I now see only dimly, nevertheless I see that you are preparing for me a far better place than this. Lord, help me to keep my eyes fixed on this truth and give me the strength to not be distracted by the circumstances swirling around me.

Amen!

———

Six
What's Our Focus?

*"So we fix our eyes not on what is seen,
but what is unseen"*

Has anyone ever "fixed you with a stare"? If so, you know it's not just any old look. It's not a glance. It's not a casual observation. It's not a nod in your direction to acknowledge your presence. It's an eye lock, a deliberate and prolonged gaze that shuts out every other possible focus of attention. It's as if a shaft of carbon steel has been welded from another person's eyes to yours.

In much that way, I used to lock on my catcher's glove when I was pitching in the major leagues. Batters were merely distractions, especially if they were good hitters. My goal was to so focus on my catcher's glove that I wouldn't even see the batter.

It is this kind of stare we are instructed to level at the unseen things of God. Countless distractions will clamor for our attention, trying feverishly to seduce our eyes to drift in their direction, but God urges us to fix our gaze on his eternal truths. Only in that way will we be enabled to look past the vicious cuts life takes at us and wind up with a big "W" on our final scorecard.

Keep Your Eye on the Boss, Not on the Ball

Whoever loves money never has money enough; whoever loves wealth is never satisfied with his income. . . .
The sleep of a laborer is sweet, whether he eats little or
much, but the abundance of a rich man permits him no
sleep. . . . Naked a man comes from his mother's womb,
and as he comes, so he departs.
—Ecclesiastes 5:10, 12, 15

Keep your eye on the ball." That's one of the cardinal rules of baseball, whether you're batting or fielding. A variation says, "Look the ball into your glove." The idea in both cases is that disaster strikes when you fail to maintain visual contact with the ball.

Wouldn't you know it? When it comes to the spiritual realm, this advice is exactly backward. In the arena of the spirit, if you maintain visual contact with visible realities and take your eyes *off* what is unseen, you're in trouble. It sounds a little confusing, but really, it's not.

God tells us in his Word that if we insist on fixing our eyes on what is seen—on houses, cars, groceries, clothes, jewelry, furniture, vacuum cleaners, washing machines, cellular phones—we will never be able to "hit the ball" in the spiritual realm. We will continue to swing and swing and miss and miss until we're out of outs and the game is over.

That is why Ecclesiastes (not one of the more upbeat books in the Bible, but certainly one of the more direct) says things like "whoever loves money never has money enough" and "the abundance of a rich man permits him no sleep." When you're consumed by the material, it returns the favor and consumes you. Still, it's pretty easy when you're a physical being to emphasize the physical and minimize the spiritual. Are we supposed to ignore the physical completely?

Certainly there's nothing wrong with taking care of the items God has entrusted to our care. In fact, none other than the apostle Paul warns us, "If anyone does not provide for his relatives, and especially for his immediate family, he has denied the faith and is worse than an unbeliever" (1 Tim. 5:8). That's a pretty harsh judgment. In other words, the person who neglects the physical *necessities* of life because he wants to be "spiritual" is not a great saint but a great fool. Mature spirituality does not mean that we lie down and pray and expect God to feed, clothe, and house us through some miraculous blast of cosmic energy. It means, rather, that we work hard with our hands to care for our loved ones even as we exercise our spirit to grow in faith and godliness. We dare not emphasize the first in such a way that we neglect the second. We should never allow material concerns to monopolize our time and consume us to the point that all we do is work and give our time to them.

I'll never forget October 17, 1989. That's the day a severe earthquake rocked most of northern California, including the San Francisco Bay area where I was participating in the third game of the World Series in Candlestick Park. I vividly remember feeling the strength and power of that quake. The Bay area was devastated and the World Series was delayed several weeks due to the damage.

The earthquake's epicenter was located in the mountains just east of the coastal city of Santa Cruz. About seventy percent of the city's downtown area was completely destroyed by the quake, which registered 7.1 on the Richter scale.

Before the earthquake hit, I had been scheduled to speak November 1 at an annual prayer breakfast for the city of Santa Cruz. Ticket sales before the earthquake were modest; after the devastation there was standing room only. The citizens of Santa Cruz were frightened and were turning to God for answers.

I will always remember a personal story that a man from the crowd told me that day. He said that fifteen years before the quake, he and his wife had bought their "dream home" in Santa Cruz. They spent fifteen years of their lives putting all their time, money, and efforts into that home. Many times, he chose to stay home on Sunday mornings and work on his house instead of going to church. His home had become his god. But during the earthquake, in a short fifteen seconds—one second for every year he spent worshiping his "god"—his home was completely destroyed.

If only he had heeded Paul's words in 1 Timothy 6:6–10: "But godliness with contentment is great gain. For we brought nothing into the world, and we can take nothing out of it. But if we have food and clothing, we will be content with that. People who want to get rich [or who want to build their own personal castles] fall into temptation and a trap and into many foolish and harmful desires that plunge men into ruin and destruction. For the love of money is a root of all kinds of evil."

We cannot afford to fix our eyes on what is seen. It doesn't last and it doesn't satisfy. In fifteen seconds it can all be gone. "Naked a man comes from his mother's womb, and as he comes, so he departs." We aren't meant for this world and our hearts will only be broken if we try to possess any little piece of it. So what should we pursue? "Godliness with contentment," Paul suggests. In that there is "great gain," not heartbreaking loss.

So don't break your heart. Go for gain and not for loss. Keep your eye on the Boss, not the ball, and you'll be OK. That's the way they do it in the *real* major leagues.

A Long Way from Nonsense

Let us fix our eyes on Jesus, the author and perfecter
of our faith, who for the joy set before him endured
the cross, scorning its shame, and sat down at
the right hand of the throne of God.

—Hebrews 12:2

Before I became a Christian, a verse that encouraged me to "fix my eyes on Jesus" sounded like nothing short of nonsense. In the first place, could anyone prove that this Jesus ever really existed? In the second place, if he did exist, he's dead by now, so who cares? And third, if he did exist and if he did still have meaning for people today, how do you fix your eyes on a person you can't see? Do you sort of stare at a corner and hope he's there?

A book by Josh McDowell called *The Resurrection Factor* was one of the chief tools God used to help me answer these questions and bring me to faith in the risen Christ. I quickly learned that no one seriously questioned the existence of Jesus any longer for the simple reason that more evidence supports his existence as a real person of history than exists for almost any other major figure of antiquity. If you want to doubt the existence of Jesus, you had better also disbelieve in Julius Caesar, Plato, Confucius, and a host of others. I wasn't ready to do that.

But so what if he existed? How did that affect me? This is where Josh's book was most helpful. By citing expert testimony after expert testimony and by presenting fact after fact, he proved to me that Jesus not only lived in Palestine two thousand years ago but that he rose again from the grave after being crucified! He cited scholars like B. F. Westcott who said, "Taking all the evidence together, it is not too much to say that there is no historic incident better or more variously supported than the resurrection of Christ."[1]

I don't have space here to review all the reasons Josh's book was so compelling to me—you can read it for yourself. I wish you would. The short version is, he convinced me that Jesus had risen from the dead; I could not deny the resurrection of Christ. And because he rose from the grave, I could accept his words and claims in the Bible.

Josh did more, however, than convince me that a historical event took place. He also showed me why it was important:

> George Eldon Ladd concludes: "The only rational explanation for these historical facts is that God raised Jesus in bodily form." A believer in Jesus Christ today can have complete confidence, as did the first Christians, that his faith is based not on myth or legend but on the solid historical fact of the risen Christ and the empty tomb.
>
> Most important of all, the individual believer can experience the power of the risen Christ in his life today. First of all, he can know that his sins are forgiven. Second, he can be assured of eternal life and his own resurrection from the grave. Third, he can be released from a meaningless and empty life and be transformed into a new creature in Jesus Christ.[2]

Believe me, I wanted all of those three things! I wanted to know my sins were forgiven. I wanted to be assured of eternal life and my own resurrection from the grave. And I desperately wanted to be released from a meaningless and empty life! If that meant being transformed by faith into a new creature in the living Jesus Christ, then I wanted it. So I confessed my sins to God, asked for forgiveness, and placed my trust in the risen Christ. That's how I became a Christian.

As I grew in the Lord, however, the answer to that third question was still a little hazy. How do you fix your eyes on a person you can't see? Even the apostle Peter admitted, "Though you have not seen him, you love him; and even though you do not see him now, you believe in him and are filled with an inexpressible and glorious joy, for you are receiving the goal of your faith, the salvation of your souls" (1 Peter 1:8–9).

I experienced some of that "inexpressible and glorious joy"; but still, how do we today "fix our eyes on Jesus" when we can't see him? Eventually I learned the answer: through faith. It's a different kind of seeing than our physical eyes are equipped for. As Paul would write, "I pray also that the *eyes of your heart* may be enlightened in order that you may know the hope to which he has called you, the riches of his glorious inheritance in the saints, and his incomparably great power for us who believe" (Eph. 1:18–19).

That's how we fix our eyes on Jesus. We do not go looking for visions or mystical appearances or the like. Not long ago I heard about people flocking to see an image of Christ that supposedly appeared in a tortilla. No joke. That's not how we fix our eyes on Jesus. We obey that command by filling our minds with his Word, by studying the gospel accounts of his earthly life, by staying in constant touch with him through prayer, and by maintaining fellowship with his people. We remember what he suffered on our behalf to free us from our sins, and we look to his example as someone who through faith obeyed his Father's commands, even though it cost him his life, "for the joy that was set before him."

In that way we can "see Jesus, who was made a little lower than the angels, now crowned with glory and honor because he suffered death, so that by the grace of God he might taste death for everyone. In bringing many sons to glory, it was fitting that God, for whom and through whom everything exists, should make the author of their salvation perfect through suffering" (Heb. 2:9–10).

Today I don't think fixing my eyes on Jesus is nonsense. I know it's the only way I'll survive in this world. When I fix eyes of faith on my Savior, I am thrilled to see him seated "at the right hand of the throne of God." And even more remarkable than that, when I look into his Word I hear him say to me, "To him who overcomes, I will give the right to sit with me on my throne, just as I overcame and sat down with my Father on his throne" (Rev. 3:21). I want to overcome, and the way to do that is by fixing my eyes on Jesus. It's not such a bad sight: Jesus, his Father, and me. You know, I think I could get used to sitting on a throne.

Christ's grave was the birthplace of an indestructible belief

that death is vanquished and there is life eternal.

—*Adolph Harnack*

Notes

1. Josh McDowell, *More Than a Carpenter* (Wheaton, Ill.: Tyndale House, 1977), 96–97.
2. Ibid., 98.

Seeing Is Not Always Believing

Though you have not seen him, you love him; and even though
you do not see him now, you believe in him and are filled with
an inexpressible and glorious joy, for you are receiving the
goal of your faith, the salvation of your souls.

—1 Peter 1:8–9

I think the old saying "seeing is believing" is vastly overrated. I know I'm swimming against the tide here and that our culture has elevated this proverb almost to the level of sacred truth. But I don't think it covers nearly as many bases as its press reports claim. Let me explain.

It's not at all uncommon to hear someone say he can't believe in God because he's never seen him. Remember the famous line of the first Soviet cosmonaut in space? God must not exist, because he didn't see him up there. This kind of logic (or illogic) has been increasing in the last several years. "If I can't see God, I won't believe in him." Seeing is believing, they say.

Oh, really?

I doubt you've seen air, but would you try to live in a vacuum? I doubt you've seen the center of the earth, but would you bet there isn't one? I doubt you've seen sound waves, but would you cut off your ears?

The fact is, we believe in a lot of things that we've never seen and don't understand. Did you know there are four basic forces in the physical world? Scientists talk about gravity, the electromagnetic force, the strong force, and the weak force. Everybody knows about gravity; it's what keeps us from flying off into space. Electromagnetism includes forms of energy like light and radio waves. The strong and the weak forces are found in the interior of atoms and keep them from blowing apart.

Just because we have names for these things, however, doesn't mean we've either seen them or understand them. In fact, we don't know much more about any of these forces than we ever have, at least in terms of why they act as they do. What exactly is gravity? How does it work? Why does it work? If we understood that, we'd all be flying around in antigravity vehicles, but so far I've seen them only in the comics pages and in science fiction.

So does that mean I stop believing in gravity? Hardly. I believe in it because I can see its effects all around me. *And that is exactly why I also believe in God.* I have never seen God in the direct physical sense, but I have seen his handiwork—especially in my current line of work. I see him every day in the lives of people in pain. In October 1982 the following quote from Joni Eareckson Tada appeared on the cover of *Moody Monthly*:

> People with disabilities are God's best visual aid to demonstrate who he really is. His power shows up best in weakness. And who by the world's standards is weaker than the mentally or physically disabled? As the world watches, these people persevere. They live, love, trust, and obey him. Eventually the world is forced to say, "How great their God must be to inspire this kind of loyalty."

But as good as that proof is, the ultimate argument for the existence of God is the life, death, and resurrection of the Lord Jesus.

As the writer of the book of Hebrews said, "The Son is the radiance of God's glory and the exact representation of his being" (Heb. 1:3). Jesus himself claimed, "If you really knew me, you would know my Father as well. . . . Anyone who has seen me has seen the Father" (John 14:7, 9). Jesus was God's visual aid to the world to demonstrate what God is like. Yet he knew that people would not believe just because he said so. That is why he also declared, "Believe me when I say that I am in the Father and the Father is in me; or at least believe on the evidence of the miracles themselves" (John 14:11).

"Now you're talking," someone says. "Miracles—that's what I need to see. If I could just see a miracle, then I'd believe. But not before."

Oh, really? Jesus was God's audiovisual aid to the world, yet many people saw him and still disbelieved.

They saw the Lord of glory in human flesh and called it a baby in a manger.

They saw spectacular miracles and called them tricks.

They saw powerful exorcisms and called them devilish.

They saw divine wisdom in action and called it crazy.

They saw Lazarus raised from the dead and called for his murder.

They saw the Lamb of God and called out, "Crucify! Crucify!"

There is a reason the resurrected Jesus said to "doubting" Thomas, "blessed are those who have not seen and yet have believed" (John 20:29). He didn't mean that the less evidence there is, the more we ought to believe. He had produced more than enough evidence. Thomas had been with Jesus for more than three years and had seen the miracles and the exorcisms and the divine wisdom in action. He had heard the Lord predict both his crucifixion and his resurrection. All the necessary evidence was there; the only thing lacking was faith. And as Hebrews 11:6 tells us, "without faith it is impossible to please God, because anyone who comes to him must believe that he exists and that he rewards those who earnestly seek him."

Jesus still asks that of us today. Though we have not seen him, he calls us to love him. Though we do not see him now, he calls us to believe in him (even if things aren't going so well). And the result when we do so? We are filled with "an inexpressible and glorious joy," which will culminate in the salvation of our souls.

Seeing is *not* always necessary for believing. What is necessary is trust in the One who has shown himself faithful. Placing our faith in him is not gullible, it's smart—or in Jesus' words, "blessed." And that's something I definitely want a piece of.

Just the Previews

No eye has seen,

no ear has heard,

no mind has conceived

what God has prepared for those who love him.

—*1 Corinthians 2:9*

I was thinking about my dogs the other day. Dakota and Maverick are quite a pair. One's an Australian sheepdog, the other's a golden retriever. Dakota more or less rules the roost unless he gets Maverick fired up, and then roles switch pretty quickly. We've owned them for several years now and we've grown very attached (except when they get gas; then it's, "Dakota, Maverick—OUT!" But that's another story, one that you probably don't want to hear.).

We love our dogs, but the truth is, they're not very smart. Our dogs are not capable of thought on a human level. They hear, they react, they obey (most of the time). I notice different emotions in them: love, happiness, jealousy, things like that. But it's obvious their intelligence is far below a human's. They don't understand our reasoning because we are higher beings than they are. They do not understand that the reason I don't want them in the street is that a car might hit them. They only know by trained response that they will be punished if they go there.

As I was thinking about our "boys," I realized that my relationship with them has some parallels to my relationship with God. For example, I know by now that I am often incapable of understanding God or his purposes for me. His ways are so much higher than mine. As Isaiah wrote, "'For my thoughts are not your thoughts, neither are your ways my ways,' declares the LORD. 'As the heavens are higher than the earth, so are my ways higher than your ways and my thoughts than your thoughts'" (Isa. 55:8–9). Many times I don't understand what he is doing in my life. Over time I have learned to trust him and believe that his ways for me are for my own good. I no longer get as frustrated as I used to at not being able to comprehend it all. Instead, I do my best to trust what he says.

What I have learned already about God, both through the experiences of life and through his Word, tell me that I can trust him both in the difficult spots and for my future. Repeatedly Scripture tells us to hang on, to persevere, to endure, to overcome, to remain faithful to the end. And just as often the Bible promises that we will be amply rewarded if we just stick with God. He doesn't often explain why we suffer, but then again he doesn't often give us many details on our coming reward. I think he wants us to trust him for both things.

But beyond that, I'm not sure we could understand even if he did explain it to us. I've never tried to explain to Dakota or Maverick why their meals come out of a can or what would happen to their internal organs should they collide with a moving car. They might lick my face, but they wouldn't understand. I think of an old "Far Side" cartoon by Gary Larson. The top panel is labeled "What we say to dogs" and shows an angry man threatening his dog: "Okay, Ginger! I've had it! You stay out of the garbage! Understand, Ginger? Stay out of the garbage, or else!" The bottom panel is labeled "What they hear" and features this version of the man's tirade: "blah blah GINGER blah blah blah blah blah blah blah blah GINGER blah blah blah blah blah ..." Ginger didn't get it because she isn't equipped to get it.

We're a lot like Ginger when it comes to understanding God's ways. That's why Paul quotes Isaiah so approvingly when he writes, "No eye has seen, no ear has heard, no mind has conceived what God has prepared for those who love him." We can believe him when he tells us something unimaginably good is coming our way, but we shouldn't be surprised or hurt if he doesn't give us any more details than he has. Even if he did, we wouldn't get it. I'm afraid I would hear something uncomfortably like, "blah blah blah blah DAVID blah blah blah blah blah DAVID blah blah blah blah . . ."

So until we can understand, our part is to trust and obey, just as the old hymn instructs us. When we do that, even in the hard times, we can know peace and even joy. Jim Arnoldi has discovered this to be true. Jim was given a terminal prognosis eight years ago. He has Leiomyo sarcoma, a rare and deadly cancer of the abdominal cavity. He's already a record breaker, medically speaking, having survived his disease longer than anyone in the books; but I think his spiritual progress is even more remarkable. Jim writes in a letter to one of our staff workers:

> I was reminded recently that, as Christians, we should remember that our hope is in the Promise; NOT the possibilities. To me that means that although I can have hope for better health, or a successful operation, what I need to rest in is the promise that God will sustain me in all circumstances and provide me a residence in his Presence, no matter what.
>
> I find that people tend to spend much time seeking a way *out* of a situation, rather than pleading with God for a way *through* it. Since cancer took hold of me, I found that praying for acceptance is far more comforting in the long haul. If we believe that God is Sovereign, and that all things

first pass through his fingers, then do we stand firm in our faith if we suggest that God "got the wrong guy" when trials befall us? The trials are *meant* to have application, they provide the classroom for our learning; they are the training ground for our preparedness to serve. We can gain so much from our difficulties; we shouldn't waste time looking for the way out. Haven't we heard so many say, after much suffering, "I've never felt so close to the Lord," or "My spiritual life has grown amazingly"? So, we *can* rejoice in our suffering. We *can* be thankful in all things and always!

Thankful, yes. Joyful, yes. But fully comprehending? Probably not. Someday, perhaps, we will understand why God allows some seemingly inexplicable adversities to enter our lives. First Corinthians 13:12 promises us that, when we see God "face to face" and not as in a poor reflection, we shall know fully even as we are fully known. Of course, we will never be God and there will always be divine mysteries beyond our ability to comprehend. Yet someday the things that so perplex and bother us now may become clear, resulting in a vastly greater appreciation and love for the God who has called us his own dear children.

In the meanwhile, we can rest in the sure knowledge that God is faithful and that he has something in store for us that is quite beyond our comprehension. I for one am glad he did not try to tell us more than he has. My head is already spinning at the wonders he has revealed—*and those are just the previews!*

———

Dear Lord,

Thank you for your Holy Spirit, who is here with me now as I walk this path of suffering. You said you would send me a Comforter, and you did just that. It is he who gives me the strength to keep my eyes fixed on things above. Still, I must admit there are times when it is so difficult not to think about the things of this world. It is hard for me to realize that this is not all there is to life.

Lord, I know that when I am distracted by the things of this world, I have trouble pleasing you with my life. I know that through my suffering I can be so consumed by what's happening to me that I often fail to see your comforting hand in the midst of the chaos. Lord, I want nothing more than to know that as I fix my eyes on what is unseen, I am able to see more clearly that you are at work in my life.

This issue is far too important not to take seriously. My life is at stake. Better yet, my eternal life is at stake—and Lord, there is no greater promise than the one you have given to those who place their faith and trust in Jesus: eternal life. It's incredible to think that as I fix my eyes on what is unseen—you—no matter what I face here on earth, it shall pass. And I will be with you forever!

Amen!

Seven
What Will Last for Eternity

*"For what is seen is temporary, but what is
unseen is eternal"*

This world seems solid enough. Whether we ponder the Himalayas or the Grand Canyon, the Pacific Ocean or the polar ice caps, this old earth looks like it's built to last. And it is ... to a point. It will remain until the day that "the heavens will disappear with a roar; the elements will be destroyed by fire, and the earth and everything in it will be laid bare" (2 Peter 3:10). Isaiah gives us a more poetic spin to the same event: "The earth is broken up, ... the earth is thoroughly shaken. The earth reels like a drunkard, it sways like a hut in the wind; so heavy upon it is the guilt of its rebellion that it falls—never to rise again" (Isa. 24:19–20).

Our world may seem eternal, but it's not. Its permanence is an illusion. There is a world, however, whose foundations cannot be shaken and whose streets can never be defiled. Heaven is a real place, and we're going there! It will last as long as its Architect and Maker does, and since God is eternal, so is heaven. Heaven is the place where we will live with Christ forever. And nothing is more solid than that.

I'm Going to Last Forever

The world and its desires pass away, but the
man who does the will of God lives forever.

—1 John 2:17

———————◆———————

Eternity begins now for a child of God. Have you ever thought about it like that? It's not simply that at the moment we die we exchange temporal life for eternal life. No, according to the Scriptures, if we belong to God through faith in the resurrected Christ, *right now* we have eternal life.

This idea helps to clear up a puzzling statement Jesus made in John 11. In that chapter we learn that a dear friend of Jesus is very sick and about to die. Jesus is traveling elsewhere, and the man's sisters send word that their brother is sick. They don't even ask him to come; they assume he will, once he hears of his friend's desperate condition. When Jesus hears the news, he replies, "This sickness will not end in death" (v. 4)—yet he stays put for two more days, during which time his friend Lazarus dies. When Jesus then tells his disciples that "Lazarus has fallen asleep" (v. 11), they think he means natural sleep and offer their medical opinion that sleep would be good for the man's recovery. Jesus must have shaken his head when he replied plainly, "Lazarus is dead" (v. 14).

And there is the puzzle. How could Jesus say, "This sickness will not end in death," and then just a little while later say, "Lazarus is dead"?

The answer is found in 1 John 2:17. When John writes, "The world and its desires pass away, but the man who does the will of God lives forever," he means that eternal life is not given to believers at the moment of their death but rather is theirs from the moment they believe. If we are people who "do the will of God," then we will live forever even if our physical bodies should pass away. We will not live forever *someday*, but we are right now, this moment, enjoying the fruits of eternal life. We will one day exchange this world for the next, but we will never again exchange temporal life for the eternal kind. If we trust in Jesus, we have already done that.

C. S. Lewis, in his inimitable way, explained his own understanding of this truth when he wrote:

> If we insist on keeping Hell (or even earth) we shall not see Heaven: if we accept Heaven we shall not be able to retain even the smallest and most intimate souvenirs of Hell. I believe, to be sure, that any man who reaches Heaven will find that what he abandoned (even in plucking out his right eye) was precisely nothing: that the kernel of what he was really seeking even in his most depraved wishes will be there, beyond expectation, waiting for him in "the High Countries." . . . I think earth, if chosen instead of Heaven, will turn out to have been, all along, only a region in Hell: and earth, if put second to Heaven, to have been from the beginning a part of Heaven itself.[1]

But the best explanation, of course, comes from the lips of our Savior himself. When he finally arrived in Bethany where Lazarus and his two sisters had lived, he was greeted by the words, "Lord, if you had been here, my brother would not have died" (John 11:21). Martha was grief stricken and couldn't help but pour out her anguish when she at last caught sight of Jesus (her sister, Mary, would do the same thing a little later). And how did Jesus respond? With some of the most powerful, encouraging words possible: "I am the resurrection and the life. He who believes in me will live, even though he dies; and whoever lives and believes in me will never die. Do you believe this?" (vv. 25–26).

I wonder—do *we* believe this? Do we believe that if we have placed our faith in Jesus, we already have eternal life? Do we believe that even if our bodies should stop breathing, we will never die? Do we believe this?

Martha did believe it. Her sister Mary also believed it. And you know the rest of the story—Jesus raises Lazarus from the grave after four days of entombment so that everyone else would have reason to believe it as well. But where is Lazarus today? Have you seen him lately? I haven't. And I know you haven't, either, because his body died a second time a little later on. He might even have been murdered, because John 12:10–11 tells us, "the chief priests made plans to kill Lazarus as well [as Jesus], for on account of him many of the Jews were going over to Jesus and putting their faith in him."

And yet Lazarus *never* died, even though his vital signs flat-lined twice (the second time, for good). How can we say this and still be completely accurate? *Because eternity begins here and now for a child of God.*

In commenting on the passage in 1 John, *The Bible Knowledge Commentary* states, "A person whose character and personality are shaped by obedience to God will not be affected by the passing away of the world and its vain desires. It is a Johannine way of saying, 'Only one life, 'twill soon be past; only what's done for Christ will last.'"[2]

I don't mean to meddle with old and cherished sayings, but I think the one Walvoord and Zuck quote above can be improved upon. If I were given the chance, I'd amend it to read, "Only one life, 'twill soon be past; yet those who are Christ's will always last."

OK, so I'm no poet. But you don't have to be good at crafting verses to understand that eternal life is ours, at this moment. It can't be taken away and it will never become more everlasting than it is right now. My body may die, but I never will. I'm already at one end of a line that stretches, unbroken, into infinity. Any way you slice it, that means I'm going to last forever. And so will you, as long as Jesus is at the other end of the line.

Notes

1. C. S. Lewis, *The Great Divorce* (Toronto: Macmillan, 1946), 6–7.
2. John F. Walvoord and Roy B. Zuck, *The Bible Knowledge Commentary* (Wheaton, Ill.: Scripture Press, Victor Books, 1983), 891.

Welcome Home

All these people were still living by faith when they died.
They did not receive the things promised; they only saw them
and welcomed them from a distance. And they admitted that
they were aliens and strangers on earth. People who say
such things show that they are looking for a country of their
own. If they had been thinking of the country they had left,
they would have had opportunity to return. Instead, they were
longing for a better country—a heavenly one. Therefore
God is not ashamed to be called their God, for he has
prepared a city for them.
—*Hebrews 11:13–16*

———————

The other day I was reading through Hebrews 11, the famous
"Faith Hall of Fame," and a thought struck that had never
before occurred to me. It wasn't a pleasant thought; in fact, it made
me shudder. Usually, when I walk through this part of Scripture, I
leave refreshed, encouraged, and strengthened. Yet this time a
question popped into my head that filled me with none of those
things. Here's the question:

Wouldn't it be awful if God were ashamed to be called my God?

I don't like to meditate on that thought, but perhaps it would
be good for us to think about it for just a little while. The question
came to me after reading verse 16 of Hebrews 11: "Instead, they

were longing for a better country—a heavenly one. Therefore God is not ashamed to be called their God, for he has prepared a city for them." The writer was describing a number of famous saints from the Old Testament who lived for God through faith. Often they gave up a lot to do it. They left behind countries, homes, relatives, jobs, possessions, fields, status. They "admitted they were aliens and strangers on earth." Their hopes were not locked onto anything here below, but were fixed on things above. They longed for another place, for heaven. And *that* is why the writer says God was not ashamed to be called their God.

So then, I thought, *the reverse must also be true. Perhaps he is ashamed of his people when they get too comfortable in this world and don't much anticipate the world to come. I wonder—is he ashamed of me?*

I don't want God to be ashamed of me. I don't want him to blush when I come into the room. I don't want him to point me out to one of his angels and say, "Yes, he's one of mine, even though he doesn't act like it." So I'm glad I don't have to be uncertain about the answer to my last question: *Is he ashamed of me?* The answer is completely under my control. It all depends on whether I consider myself an alien and a stranger in this world and anxiously look forward to heaven. If that is my attitude, then I'll also live like it. Then I'll know that God is not ashamed to be called my God, and the proof will be the "city" he is preparing for me.

As children of God, we are citizens of heaven. Earth is no longer our home; we long for heaven. The apostle Paul wrote, "But our citizenship is in heaven. And we eagerly await a Savior from there, the Lord Jesus Christ" (Phil. 3:20). Peter looked at it from another angle and said, "Dear friends, I urge you, as aliens and strangers in the world, to abstain from sinful desires, which war against your soul" (1 Peter 2:11). Both men were echoing the message of Hebrews 11.

Oh, how this conviction should change the way we live right now! It did for Jessica Eggert, a ten-year-old girl who was diagnosed with osteogenic sarcoma, a rare cancer that is fatal if not caught soon enough. In Jessica's case, it wasn't. Her father tells the story:

> I don't know exactly how Jessica came to grasp the reality of heaven, but she certainly did. It must have been in Sunday School that she learned the truth of 2 Peter 3:8, "But do not forget this one thing, dear friends: With the Lord a day is like a thousand years, and a thousand years are like a day." I think our talks about the deaths of "Grandpa" Towne and "Grandma" Neva, "Papa" Ed and "Grandma" Doe, the dear saints who had befriended our children, added to her realization that heaven is a very real place. I believe the assurance of their presence in heaven did much to remove her fear. She already knew people who were in heaven and knew that they were waiting for her.
>
> By God's grace and many answered prayers, Jessica lived with her cancer for three and one-half years, although we had been told it would kill her within two to three months. Through her whole struggle—the horrible chemotherapy, the final weakening stage—her confidence in what lay ahead for her never wavered. I was amazed by how real heaven was to her. I was inspired by her complete peace. I found encouragement in her lack of fear or dread. Our hope, our comfort, and our strength for grieving were immeasurably enhanced by the powerful simplicity of her faith.
>
> We will never forget our last evening with her. She was obviously near death and leaned across my chest. "I'm ready to go now, Daddy," she said.
>
> "Do you mean to heaven?"
>
> "Yes, Daddy. I'm ready to go over there."

And go there she did, a few hours after slipping peacefully into a coma. She was barely a teenager, but she understood better than most of us what A. E. Brumley meant when he wrote:

This world is not my home, I'm just a passing through,
My treasures are laid up somewhere beyond the blue;
The angels beckon me from heaven's open door,
And I can't feel at home in this world anymore.[1]

Jessica shared that sentiment. She didn't feel at home in this world anymore, either, but she certainly felt at ease when a very unashamed God beckoned her to her new home in her new city and said joyfully, "Welcome home, Jessica. It just wouldn't be heaven without you."

Note

1. A. E. Brumley, "This World Is Not My Home" (Glendale, Calif.: Praise Book Publications, 1951), 111. Used by permission.

Our Father's House

"Do not let your hearts be troubled. Trust in God; trust also in me. In my Father's house are many rooms; if it were not so, I would have told you. I am going there to prepare a place for you. And if I go and prepare a place for you, I will come back and take you to be with me that you also may be where I am."

—John 14:1–3

So many things can trouble our hearts. Unpaid bills. A frightening medical prognosis. Loss of a job. The death of a loved one. Upcoming surgery. An unexpected move. An argument with a close friend. A savage rumor. A church dispute.

The world is full of "heart troublers," and it always will be. Yet Jesus does not want our hearts to remain troubled. And he does not expect us to deal with those troubles so much by ignoring them as by turning toward him. As he said to his anxious disciples in John 14:1, "Trust in God; trust also in me."

Why were the disciples so anxious? It was something he had said to them, the sound of which they didn't like at all. He had declared, "My children, I will be with you only a little longer. You will look for me, and just as I told the Jews, so I tell you now: Where I am going, you cannot come" (John 13:33). These words put the disciples into a tailspin, Peter most of all. So as the leader of the twelve, he asked Jesus, "Lord, where are you going?" (v. 36).

And that's when Jesus told them about heaven.

There's nothing escapist about pondering heaven. Jesus told us about it not so that we could escape from our troubles but so that we could better endure them. He wants us to think about heaven, especially when anxious thoughts seize our hearts. Although we won't enjoy its full benefits until we arrive, even now we can allow its atmosphere to fill our lungs with hope. That's what some young friends of mine did recently when I asked them to tell me what they thought heaven would be like. Here's what they said:

> The best part of heaven is the party Jesus is going to give us. Lots of babies will be in heaven. If we need our dolls in heaven, Jesus will have them there.
>
> Micah Leake, age 3

> There are roads of gold, gates of pearl, and after you have walked through the gates of pearl, I think you might see a humongous throne. I think the throne is made out of bricks of gold and outlined with pearls, decorated with emeralds— maybe even rubies! I don't know if I'm right, but I do know you will have to have bare feet.
>
> Emily Edwards, age 7

> God says that heaven is perfect for everyone, and we each have our own idea of what perfect is. My dad died, so part of my perfect heaven would be to have my dad there with me. Best of all, we could see God whenever we wanted.
>
> Taylor Andrews, age 13

> Heaven will be like living in the clouds with Christ and you can roller blade on streets of gold. Peter will give you

fishing lessons. We'll all be able to fly. We'll play tag in the sky. The trees will be made of gold and the leaves of silver. My point is, heaven is going to be wonderful!

Isaac Allen Jones, age 11

I think heaven would have fences in it with strawberries. David who fighted Goliath would be there too. I think heaven would have blueberries and gold in it. Old people will be there and God's angels. There also will be a big, big feast that keeps everybody full.

Andrew Edwards, age 3

Heaven will be the greatest place ever, but mainly because Jesus will be there. To get to this great place, though, you must believe in Christ our Lord.

Heather Knepper, age 11

Heaven is a place where you can just have fun. It's a place where you can see your friends again. I'll be happy. I'll be able to put unpleasant times, bad days, seizure medicine . . . all that stuff behind me.

Benjamin Leake, age 10

Thinking about heaven is a great way to put "all that stuff" behind us, at least for a little while. That's why Jesus told us about it. You know, he didn't have to tell us about heaven—it could have remained his big secret—but he wanted us to know what was coming so that we could deal with what is now.

He also wanted us to know that, when the time is right, there won't be any problem in getting us to heaven. He wouldn't entrust this task to some third-level angel or to some celestial scoop that would mechanically pluck us out of earth and dump us in paradise. He wanted us to know that he would come for us himself: "And if I go and prepare a place for you, I will come back and take you to be with me that you also may be where I am."

When will this happen? We don't know. When the disciples asked him this very question, he said things like, "It is not for you to know the times or dates the Father has set by his own authority" (Acts 1:7) and "Keep watch, because you do not know on what day your Lord will come" (Matt. 24:42) and "So you also must be ready, because the Son of Man will come at an hour when you do not expect him" (Matt. 24:44).

We don't know when he's coming back to take us home. But we don't have to know. What we must do is be ready and keep watch. Our guided excursion to heaven could take place even before you finish reading this sentence (or even before I finish writing it—well, I guess not). Heaven is certain, and so is our Lord's promise to take us there, whenever the Father decides it's time to fulfill that promise.

Whooosh!

———

Life Is a Dream and Heaven's Reality

And I heard a loud voice from the throne saying, "Now the dwelling of God is with men, and he will live with them. They will be his people, and God himself will be with them and be their God. He will wipe every tear from their eyes. There will be no more death or mourning or crying or pain, for the old order of things has passed away." He who was seated on the throne said, "I am making everything new!"

—Revelation 21:3–5

Heaven. As the song says, "Life is a dream, and heaven's reality." This earth is not our true home, heaven is. And until we let go of impossible hopes for this world and grip tightly the certain hope of the world to come, we will never be able to fully appreciate the love of God poured out on our behalf. As Joni Eareckson Tada wrote in her wonderful book *Heaven: Your Real Home*:

> Broken homes, broken bodies, and broken hearts crush our illusions that earth can keep its promises, that it can really satisfy us. Only the hope of heaven can truly move our passions off this world, which God knows could never fulfill us anyway, and fix them where they will find their glorious fulfillment.

When we finally realize that the hopes we have cherished will never come true, that a loved one is gone from this life forever, that a child's diagnosis of inoperable cancer will never change, or that we will never be as successful as we had once imagined, our sights are lifted heavenward.

My hopes of running through earthly meadows and splashing my feet in a stream will never come true on earth, but it will in heaven. My dream of hugging a loved one and actually *feeling* his or her embrace will never come true on earth, but it will when we stand together before Jesus.[1]

We are headed for heaven! We have a permanent home waiting for us in a land where "there will be no more death or mourning or crying or pain." God will no longer seem to be a resident of a far-off place, but he himself will live among us and will wipe every tear from our eyes. We will drink without cost from the spring of the water of life and will give overflowing thanks that the old order of things has passed away, never to return and trouble us again.

The Bible doesn't tell us much about heaven, but what we are told takes our breath away. Even so, just because we know so little about it, questions arise: "Will I be bored there?" "Will I know people there?" "Will I be sad because someone I love isn't there?" These three questions, especially, often come up when we speak with people who know they are about to take up residence in glory. They are glad to be going home, but . . .

So let's briefly tackle these three questions and see what we might be able to discover. If heaven is such an attractive, glorious place, then three little questions like these shouldn't be able to tarnish its brilliance for even a twinkling of an eye.

Will I be bored in heaven? Not unless you think boredom is "better" than anything earth has to offer now. *Better* is the key word throughout the book of Hebrews. Chapter 11 lists an honor roll of great people of faith from the Old Testament who often left their native countries to serve God because "they were longing for a *better* country—a heavenly one" (v. 16). And while all of them were commended for their faith, none of them received what had been promised to them. Why not? "God had planned something *better* for us so that only together with us would they be made perfect" (v. 40). And where would that happen? In heaven!

Think of the best day you've ever had. Remember the joy? The excitement? The thrill? The sheer happiness that welled up in your heart and burst into uncontrollable laughter and ear-to-ear smiles? Well, that was good—but heaven is better. So if that's boredom, bring it on!

Will I know people in heaven? Some folks are afraid that when they get to heaven, they won't recognize anyone. They're fearful that they won't know their husband of thirty-five years without a name tag pinned to his robe. But I doubt that will be a problem. Not only will you know your loved ones, it's likely you'll know everyone else, too, even without an introduction.

Luke 9:28–36 tells the story of the Transfiguration, which Jesus described as a preview of heaven. Peter, James, and John accompanied Jesus to a mountain to pray, and while their Master was praying, "The appearance of his face changed, and his clothes became as bright as a flash of lightning. Two men, Moses and Elijah, appeared in glorious splendor, talking with Jesus." Peter immediately recognized the visitors and blurted out, "Master, it is good for us to be here. Let us put up three shelters—one for you, one for Moses and one for Elijah." Mark, in his account, says Peter didn't know what to say because he was so frightened (Mark 9:5–6). Yet how did Peter know Jesus was flanked by Moses and Elijah? These men had lived hundreds of years before Peter's time, so he had never met them.

There were no photographs in those days, no artist's sketches. How did he recognize them? He just knew, that's all.

The Transfiguration was a preview of heaven, and in heaven there will be no need for introductions. We'll know everyone the moment we see them, just as Peter instantly knew Moses and Elijah. One difference, though—we won't be afraid.

Will I be sad because someone I love isn't in heaven? When God says he will wipe away *every* tear from our eyes, he means it. That means there won't be any sadness of any kind in heaven. How can this be?

C. S. Lewis tried to explain some of this in his fascinating little book *The Great Divorce*, in which an imaginary busload of people from hell takes an excursion to heaven with the promise that they can stay if they want to. Few make the choice. One conversation takes place between a redeemed woman and her unsaved husband. He cannot understand how she can seem so happy when he is not there. She tells him that he could choose, even now, to experience the joys of heaven, but that she cannot feel sorrow because

> "There *are* no miseries here.... Here is joy that cannot be shaken. Our light can swallow up your darkness: but your darkness cannot now infect our light.... Can you really have thought that love and joy would always be at the mercy of frowns and sighs? Did you not know they were stronger than their opposites?"[2]

I hope these answers help. They help me. Yet in the end, we must leave our questions behind and cling to the One who promises to give us not every answer, but a home with him in heaven, forever. That's a promise I can live with, as well as a promise I can live for.

I'm going to heaven! *And I hope to see you there with me.*

Heaven

Heaven cannot be described
in words by mortal man.
And though the artists do their best,
it can't be drawn in pen.
Imaginations, though they try,
fall short in every way.
For only God can make a place
where all will long to stay.

Carla Muir

———

Dear Lord,

For the most part, my life has revolved around what I can see. I know I am not alone in this. Often I feel like doubting Thomas, who had to see with his own eyes and touch with his own hands before he would believe.

But Lord, do you know something? As I move closer to you through all I've been experiencing, the truth is that your Word stands the test of time. It is my comfort, my strength, my encouragement, my hope. It expresses all that you are and just how much you love me.

Here's the bottom line: Life is a dream and heaven's reality! I thank you that as a child of yours, heaven is my home. As the psalmist said, "My comfort in my suffering is this: Your promise preserves my life." Lord, you have given me an incredible gift, a gift I don't deserve. And yet you give it freely! For that I am eternally grateful.

Lord, my life is in your hands. I know there will be times when I will be shaken (like now), but through it all I know you will be there to help me. Thank you for the wonderful encouragement you have given me through your Word, from the gentle touch of a family member, and from the comforting embrace of a friend. All this reveals just how real you are.

Abba, Father, Daddy, my prayer for all of us is that as we travel on this journey of life, we would be able to say with confidence, as Paul did, that going home means going to God. Help us to see that heaven is a place where, for all eternity, we can heap praises upon our infinitely precious God. And may that cause us to yearn for glory. For heaven. For paradise.

FOR HOME!

Amen!

Notes

1. Joni Eareckson Tada, *Heaven: Your Real Home* (Grand Rapids: Zondervan, 1995), 96.

2. C. S. Lewis, *The Great Divorce* (Toronto: Macmillan, 1946), 112.

Epilogue

The Final Steps Toward Home

Reading books and living life have at least two things in common. First, they are both journeys: books, like life, feature hills and plains, valleys and mountains, rivers and lakes, seas and oceans. Second, good books and lives well-spent hold this in common: Both are headed somewhere wonderful.

We hope that as you have reached the end of this book, you have enjoyed the journey. It has been our pleasure to act as your guides, pointing you to some of the great encouragement found in God's Word. And we hope that we have provided you with enough glimpses of the gracious terrain of Scripture that you have ended your journey in a wonderful place.

But even more important than that, our earnest desire is that your personal life-journey is full of the love and peace of God. Whether you are currently walking through a dark valley or raising your arms in triumph on a mountain summit, our prayer is that the Lord Jesus is your constant Companion and Guide. And we especially pray that the promise of heaven occupies a treasured place in your heart, that you know without a doubt that when your life on earth is finished, you have a home in glory waiting for you.

Before we take the final steps toward home, however, we must live life here below. God wants us to live our lives in truth and in hope, recognizing our struggles now but living by faith as we look forward to a sure eternity in paradise. As they say, "Life is hard, but God is good."

Our final word to you is the same as our initial word: Do not lose heart! We hope that if these pages have provided any encouragement for you, you'll revisit them and reread them often. It would encourage us to know that our labors have not been in vain. Yet none of us must ever forget where our only real, permanent, strong, and invincible hope lies. As a far greater author wrote long ago:

So then, brothers, stand firm and hold to the teachings we passed on to you, whether by word of mouth or by letter. May our Lord Jesus Christ himself and God our Father, who loved us and by his grace gave us eternal encouragement and good hope, encourage your hearts and strengthen you in every good deed and word. (2 Thess. 2:15–16)

About Dave Dravecky's Outreach of Hope

On the ceiling of the Sistine Chapel is found one of Michelangelo's most famous paintings. God is shown reaching down from heaven, hand extended, to touch the outstretched hand of man.

The natural human response to pain and suffering is to do just the opposite, to recoil and retreat in fear and anger. When we suffer, the very thing we need most—the love and intimacy of God—can seem farthest from us. Our goal as encouragers is to gently and lovingly pick up the weary arm and lift it heavenward, connecting or reconnecting it with its source of joy, peace, and eternal life.

Because of the complexity of human nature, the position and flexibility of that arm can vary greatly from person to person. Therefore, we rely totally on the work of the Holy Spirit to give us the discernment and wisdom to know how best to accomplish this goal.

The mission of Dave Dravecky's Outreach of Hope is to offer hope and encouragement through Jesus Christ to those suffering from cancer or amputation. Our mission is accomplished by providing:

- *Resources* that provide guidance and encouragement to cancer patients, amputees, and their families. The Encourager magazine is our primary resource for communicating encouragement and hope. It is sent to thousands of families, churches, and health care providers throughout the country. In addition, more than 100 other resources are available to meet the unique needs of those who suffer. These include resources for caregivers, families, and children.

- *Referrals* of a non-medical nature from a database of national organizations that can provide practical assistance and resources for the afflicted individual or family.
- *Prayer Support* for patients and their families through daily intercessory prayer teams, individual phone prayer, and our nationwide prayer warrior ministry. Connecting people to God through prayer is at the heart of what we believe and do.
- *Support Materials* for churches, health professionals, and individuals who work with cancer patients, amputees, and their families.
- *Teaching & Training* for those want to extend encouragement but need practical advice and motivation to reach out to those who are hurting. Speaking to audiences in churches and hospitals throughout the country, Dave and Jan share their journey and the lessons they learned in the valley of adversity. They challenge listeners to rise to the call of touching and changing the lives of those who suffer.

For further information on Dave Dravecky's Outreach of Hope and its ministry to cancer patients and amputees, please write to:

For speaking engagements please contact:

Christian Speakers.com
277 Mallory Station Road, Suite 116
Franklin, TN 37067
800-220-8125
www.Christianspeakers.com

About Thomas Kinkade, Painter of Light

California artist Thomas Kinkade is one of the most beloved and most collected contemporary artists. A modern-day impressionist, Kinkade infuses light into his paintings that evokes nostalgia, peace, and tranquillity in his works. A man of deep faith and traditional values, Thom Kinkade and his wife, Nanette, are parents of four girls.

For more information about Thomas Kinkade's limited edition art, please call 1-800-366-3733.

We want to hear from you. Please send your comments about this book to us in care of the address below. Thank you.

ZONDERVAN™

GRAND RAPIDS, MICHIGAN 49530

www.zondervan.com